W9-AZP-729

New Directions for
Institutional Research

John F. Ryan
Editor-in-Chief

Gloria Crisp
Associate Editor

The Important Role of Institutional Data in the Development of Academic Programming in Higher Education

Sydney Freeman, Jr.
Crystal Renée Chambers
Beverly Rae King
Editors

Number 168
Jossey-Bass
San Francisco

The Important Role of Institutional Data in the Development of Academic Programming in Higher Education
Sydney Freeman, Jr., Crystal Renée Chambers, Beverly Rae King (eds.)
New Directions for Institutional Research, no. 168
John F. Ryan, Editor-in-Chief
Gloria Crisp, Associate Editor

Copyright © 2016 Wiley Periodicals, Inc., A Wiley Company

All rights reserved. No part of this publication may be reproduced in any form or by any means, except as permitted under section 107 or 108 of the 1976 United States Copyright Act, without either the prior written permission of the publisher or authorization through the Copyright Clearance Center, 222 Rosewood Drive, Danvers, MA 01923; (978) 750-8400; fax (978) 646-8600. The code and copyright notice appearing at the bottom of the first page of an article in this journal indicate the copyright holder's consent that copies may be made for personal or internal use, or for personal or internal use of specific clients, on the condition that the copier pay for copying beyond that permitted by law. This consent does not extend to other kinds of copying, such as copying for general distribution, for advertising or promotional purposes, for creating collective works, or for resale. Such permission requests and other permission inquiries should be addressed to the Permissions Department, c/o John Wiley & Sons, Inc., 111 River St., Hoboken, NJ 07030; (201) 748-8789, fax (201) 748-6326, http://www.wiley.com/go/permissions.

New Directions for Institutional Research (ISSN 0271-0579, electronic ISSN 1536-075X) is part of The Jossey-Bass Higher and Adult Education Series and is published quarterly by Wiley Subscription Services, Inc., A Wiley Company, at Jossey-Bass, One Montgomery Street, Suite 1200, San Francisco, California 94104-4594 (publication number USPS 098-830). POSTMASTER: Send address changes to New Directions for Institutional Research, Jossey-Bass, One Montgomery Street, Suite 1200, San Francisco, California 94104-4594.

Individual Subscription Rate (in USD): $89 per year US/Can/Mex, $113 rest of world; institutional subscription rate: $341 US, $381 Can/Mex, $415 rest of world. Single copy rate: $29. Electronic only–all regions: $89 individual, $341 institutional; Print & Electronic–US: $98 individual, $410 institutional; Print & Electronic–Canada/Mexico: $98 individual, $450 institutional; Print & Electronic–Rest of World: $122 individual, $484 institutional.

Editorial Correspondence should be sent to John F. Ryan at jfryan@uvm.edu.

New Directions for Institutional Research is indexed in *Academic Search* (EBSCO), *Academic Search Elite* (EBSCO), *Academic Search Premier* (EBSCO), *CIJE: Current Index to Journals in Education* (ERIC), *Contents Pages in Education* (T&F), *EBSCO Professional Development Collection* (EBSCO), *Educational Research Abstracts Online* (T&F), *ERIC Database* (Education Resources Information Center), *Higher Education Abstracts* (Claremont Graduate University), *Multicultural Education Abstracts* (T&F), *Sociology of Education Abstracts* (T&F).

Cover design: Wiley
Cover Images: © Lava 4 images | Shutterstock

Microfilm copies of issues and chapters are available in 16mm and 35mm, as well as microfi che in 105mm, through University Microfilms, Inc., 300 North Zeeb Road, Ann Arbor, Michigan 48106-1346.

www.josseybass.com

THE ASSOCIATION FOR INSTITUTIONAL RESEARCH (AIR) is the world's largest professional association for institutional researchers. The organization provides educational resources, best practices, and professional development opportunities for more than 4,000 members. Its primary purpose is to support members in the process of collecting, analyzing, and converting data into information that supports decision making in higher education.

Dedication

This Special Issue of NDIR is dedicated posthumously to Lester F. Goodchild, an author of a chapter within this issue and historian of the field of higher education. Dr. Goodchild edited four books and wrote over 50 refereed articles, book chapters, book reviews, and professional publications. Beyond writing about higher education as a field, he was also a practitioner, who served and was named as Dean and Dean Emeritus of the School of Education at Santa Clara University, Interim Dean and Associate Professor of Education at the University of Denver, and Dean and Professor of the Graduate School of Education at the University of Massachusetts, Boston.

Contents

Editors' Notes

In this volume, we discuss the important ways in which institutional data inform the development and sustainability of academic programming within the academy. The central argument is the need for centrality of institutional data when making decisions related to a range of academic programs. Previous studies have addressed the need for the utilization of institutional data across a myriad of programs within colleges and universities. However, the present monograph addresses, with both depth and breadth, various types of academic programming (i.e., academic degrees, research center/institutes) at diverse institutional types including community colleges, doctoral/research universities, minority-serving, and for-profit institutions. This volume addresses an important gap within the literature by providing concrete examples of, and steps toward, how to utilize institutional data to improve academic planning and development. Chapter 1 lays the foundation, providing a conceptual model that academic leaders can use to navigate the complex, and often contentious, organizational terrain of academic program development. Chapter 2 provides three case studies of programs strategically positioned for degree distinctiveness. Chapter 3 addresses the important role that institutional research can play in the assessment and identification of strategies to address the challenge of developmental education at community colleges. Chapter 4 reviews an important aspect of academic programming that has been underresearched; that is, the relationship between institutional data and the creation and sustainability of research centers/institutes/laboratories at colleges and universities. Another growing area within higher education is the for-profit sector. Chapter 5 connects strategic planning at the institutional level to academic planning at the program level. Chapter 6 specifically reviews the case of one innovative Ph.D. program in higher education. In light of its success over the last 10 years, the author shares how institutional data helped to shape the development of the program and provide the evidential support to sustain it over this period of time. Finally, Chapter 7 synthesizes these findings, provides recommendations for institutional researchers, faculty, and academic leaders, and offers directions for future research.

Sydney Freeman, Jr.
Crystal Renée Chambers
Beverly Rae King
Editors

SYDNEY FREEMAN, JR. is an associate professor of Higher Education Leadership at the University of Idaho.

CRYSTAL RENÉE CHAMBERS is an associate professor of Educational Leadership, Higher Education Concentration at East Carolina University.

BEVERLY RAE KING is the director of Institutional Research at East Carolina University.

1

This chapter provides a conceptual model that academic leaders can use to navigate the complex, and often contentious, organizational terrain of academic program development. The model includes concepts related to the institution's external environment, as well as internal organizational structures, cultures, and politics. Drawing from the literature in management, organizational studies, and higher education, this chapter explains how various organizational configurations lead to different assumptions and practices regarding data use and program development decisions. These assumptions and practices are illustrated through a case study of the development of online programs in a community college system.

Understanding the Organizational Context of Academic Program Development

Jay R. Dee, William A. Heineman

Academic program developers are unlikely to escape expectations for data-based decision making. Given the budgetary and strategic implications of academic program development, institutions have established elaborate procedures for approving new programs and authorizing expansions and modifications of existing programs. Proposals for new academic programs may need to be supported with extensive data on the labor market demand for program graduates, as well as detailed information on the resources needed to implement the program, including faculty, facilities, and technology (Posey & Pitter, 2012). Efforts to expand or modify existing programs may need to demonstrate alignment with the curricular standards of the discipline or field of study in which the program is offered, as well as document the performance of the existing program in terms of learning outcomes, degree completion, and job placement rates. Academic program developers, therefore, may need to marshal a wide array of data, from a variety of sources, to influence the campus committees, administrative bodies, and governing boards that ultimately decide which proposals will be approved.

Academic program developers are challenged not only to get the right data to the right people; they also need to understand how those data will be

Published online in Wiley Online Library (wileyonlinelibrary.com) • DOI: 10.1002/ir.20158

used and interpreted within the organizational context of their institution (Kezar, 2014; Terenzini, 1993). The organizational context can be defined as the structural, cultural, and power configurations that characterize a particular college or university, as well as the external environment in which that institution operates (Bess & Dee, 2008). The organizational context reveals which external stakeholders are linked to the institution, which procedures are used to make decisions, which values and beliefs guide those decisions, and which groups and individuals will ultimately have the most influence on the decision outcomes (Shepherd & Rudd, 2014).

In addition to the general context of the organization, academic program developers may need to consider the specific context of the decision that they are seeking (Elbanna & Child, 2007; Papadakis, Lioukas, & Chambers, 1998). Academic program development can occur in at least three decision contexts: (a) creating a new program, (b) expanding an existing program into new subfields or new student populations, and (c) substantially modifying an existing program in terms of its curriculum, pedagogy, and/or learning outcomes. The decision context involves not only the type of decision to be made but also the scope of that decision. Scope refers to the number of departments and units in the organization that will be impacted by the decision. Does the decision affect only one academic department, or do the implications extend to include the entire institution? Furthermore, the decision context relates to the institution's history with a particular type of decision. Has this type of decision been made routinely at the institution, or is this decision considered novel and therefore somewhat risky? Finally, the decision context includes the current stage in the development of the decision. Organizational members may use data differently at various stages in the decision-making process. At early stages in the decision-making process, organizational members may use data to identify and understand problems that need to be addressed. As the process unfolds, they may use data to select among alternative courses of action. At later stages, data may be used to understand how best to implement a decision that has already been made (Mintzberg, Raisinghani, & Theoret, 1976).

The organizational context and the decision context are linked to each other. We can think of the organizational context as the map that depicts the terrain of a college or university, and the decision context as the specific route that a decision will take through that terrain. Depending upon the route, different components of the organizational context will become relevant. If a program development effort involves creating a large number of new courses, then the route will likely proceed through the institution's faculty governance committees, and academic program developers will need to be aware of how faculty from a range of disciplines will view the proposal. If the effort instead focuses on developing a new program in an emerging professional field, then the route will likely intersect with external stakeholders that have an interest in workforce development, such as the business community and government agencies.

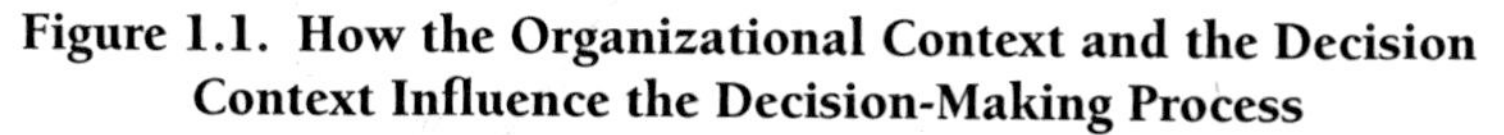

Figure 1.1. How the Organizational Context and the Decision Context Influence the Decision-Making Process

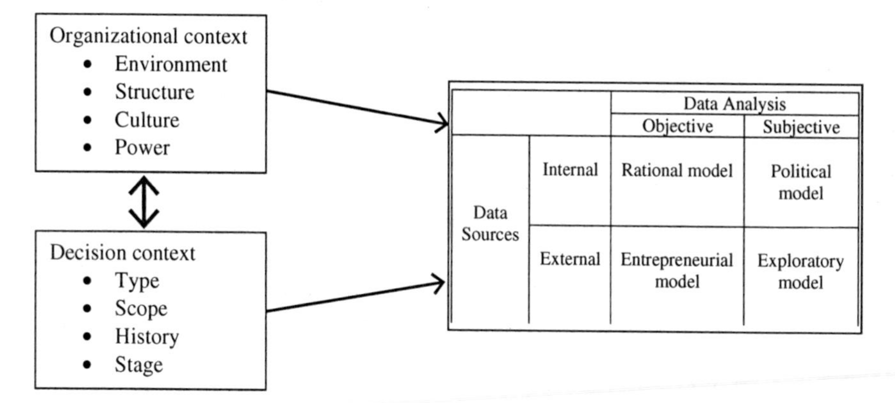

Together, the general context of the organization and the specific context of the decision will shape the decision-making process that emerges (see Figure 1.1). Based on our review of the organizational decision-making literature, we suggest that the decision process will follow one of four paths, depending on whether internal or external data are emphasized, and whether decision makers are likely to engage in objective or subjective analysis. The rational model is characterized by an objective analysis of internal data on organizational or unit performance. The entrepreneurial model also involves objective analysis, but the focus shifts to opportunities in the external environment. In contrast, the political model is based on subjective analyses that reflect the interests and power positions of internal groups. Finally, the exploratory model refers to a subjective analysis of trends and developments in the external environment. These models have different assumptions about data (objective or subjective) and assign different priorities to data sources (internal or external).

The model used for a particular decision is generally not determined by organizational members in advance of a decision; instead, the decision-making model emerges organically in relation to the interaction between the organizational context and the decision context (Mintzberg et al., 1976). For example, consider an organization that has had a long history of antagonism between faculty and administrators. In terms of the organizational context, there would be a low level of trust in the organizational culture. Furthermore, if the decision context involves issues that are considered novel and somewhat risky to the institution, then the decision-making process would likely emerge within the political model, given the focus on internal issues (risk to institution) and subjective analyses (the different views of faculty and administrators). This example is rather simplistic in that it focuses on only one component of the organizational context and only one dimension of the decision context. In fact, decision-making processes are shaped by many contextual factors that academic program developers should consider as they gather, analyze, and share data.

If academic program developers lack an understanding of the organizational context or the decision context, then their efforts may not be successful (Schmidtlein, 1999). The data that they generate may not be used or interpreted as they had expected. The accuracy of their data might be questioned. The data might not meet the expectations of key internal and external stakeholders. If the data are not shared with a key stakeholder group, then its members may complain that they have not been consulted. Furthermore, if data are not provided before key deadlines in the decision-making calendar, then decisions may stall and the "academic clock" will run out, thus postponing decisions for another academic year (Tierney, 2001).

Similar consequences may emerge if academic program developers do not understand the decision-making process that has emerged around their proposed initiative. A common issue is seeing the decision process as rational and objective, when in fact, it has emerged as subjective and political (Schmidtlein, 1999). In this scenario, academic program developers may encounter unexpected resistance or unanticipated challenges from people who interpret the data differently. Another common issue relates to seeing the decision-making process as exploratory and open to new ideas, when in fact, key decision makers have already determined what they want to do. In this scenario, academic program developers may gather data for a range of options that have already been withdrawn or were never in contention for adoption. Instead, they could use their time more effectively to gather and evaluate data on how best to implement the decisions that have already been made.

A further consideration is that the decision-making process can shift from one model to another, as the decision context changes, or as different elements of the organizational context become relevant or activated (Tarter & Hoy, 1998). An exploratory process, for example, may shift to entrepreneurial, if external trend data clarify how institutional leaders want to proceed vis-à-vis opportunities in the external environment. Likewise, a decision-making process may shift from rational to political, as groups with competing interests become aware of the resource implications associated with a particular proposal. Academic program developers always need to be attentive to the organizational context and the decision context so that they can anticipate which decision-making model will emerge.

This chapter is organized into three parts. First, the chapter uses the higher education literature to describe the key features of the organizational context that affect data and decisions regarding academic program development. Second, we delineate relevant dimensions of the decision context for academic program development. Finally, we discuss the four decision-making models that can emerge based on conditions in the organizational and decision contexts. We illustrate these four models with examples from a case study (Heineman, 2011). The case study was conducted at three community colleges, which were selected on the basis of the maturity and scope of their online programs. Interviews were conducted with eight decision makers at each college. These individuals were involved in online program development and included chief academic officers, deans, technology directors, and faculty.

Organizational Context

Many higher education scholars have suggested that institutional decision making can be improved when administrators, staff, and faculty have an understanding of the organizational context in which they operate (Bess & Dee, 2008; Birnbaum, 1988). Kezar (2014), for example, argues that learning about the contextual conditions of the institution can help change agents be more successful. Terenzini (1993) includes contextual knowledge of the organization, alongside technical skills and knowledge of higher education issues, among the key competencies for institutional researchers. Schmidtlein (1999) also suggests that institutional researchers need a keen understanding of the organizational context, and this knowledge can lead to better decisions.

Higher education institutions have unique organizational contexts that differentiate them from other types of organizations. Some of these unique features include quality assurance through accreditation and assessment, systems of shared governance, decentralized and loosely coupled organizational structures, and academic values that promote autonomy and the exploration of knowledge for its own sake (Bess & Dee, 2008; Kezar, 2014). Furthermore, colleges and universities lack clear, measurable goals, such as profit for a corporation. Instead, the goals of higher education—enhancing learning, creating new knowledge, and serving society—are somewhat vague and difficult to measure objectively. As a result, organizational members will interpret and prioritize these goals in different ways, and they will pursue activities that are consistent with their own interpretations and priorities (Temple, 2008) rather than adhere to some form of centralized coordination. Thus, the organizational context of a college or university may appear uncoordinated and somewhat chaotic to an outside observer.

Although common organizational features are found at nearly every higher education institution, the prevalence and importance of these features will vary depending upon institutional type, size, and mission (Morphew & Hartley, 2006). Shared governance committees, for example, might be more numerous in universities with large numbers of tenured faculty, and conversely, less prevalent in community colleges where most faculty are employed on a part-time basis. This section of the chapter identifies the features of the organizational context (external, structural, cultural, and power dynamics) that are most likely to influence academic program development. Although these features are discussed in general terms, readers can assess the extent to which each is important and relevant to the organizational context of the institution in which they work.

External Environment. The external environment affects academic program development primarily in the areas of government regulation, quality assurance, and market-based competition. Clark (1983) identified three external forces that impact the internal operations of colleges and universities: the government agencies that regulate higher education institutions, the academic disciplines that set standards for curriculum and learning outcomes in various fields, and the marketplace for students and other resources. This section of the chapter will examine those three forces in relation to academic program development.

Government agencies affect academic program development largely through their consumer protection function, and through policy incentives that encourage program development in certain professional fields (Wellman, 2006). Typically, before a public, private, or for-profit institution can offer a new degree program in a particular state, that state's board of higher education must approve the proposal. State boards seek to protect consumers (students) from programs that do not meet minimum standards of quality or that do not have sufficient educational resources to support student learning. Furthermore, these boards may also require institutions to provide labor market projections for graduates of the proposed program, to demonstrate that students will be able to obtain a job in the field after graduation, thus protecting students from entering programs that ultimately do not lead to careers. In addition to this regulatory function, government agencies also seek to stimulate the development of academic programs in fields deemed critical to economic development or social well-being. Federal and state government agencies have invested resources in workforce development initiatives that frequently target the STEM fields (science, technology, engineering, mathematics), as well as high-need fields that promote social well-being, such as early childhood education and health care. In addition to government agencies, foundations and other private funding sources have provided similar incentives for academic program development, again largely in the STEM fields. Private foundations, therefore, can also be viewed as a shaper of academic program development.

Through their professional societies and accreditation associations, academic disciplines have a significant impact on academic program development. Academic disciplines shape how faculty think about teaching and learning; thus, the disciplines have a significant influence on curriculum development (Becher & Trowler, 2001). This influence is formalized in fields that have accreditation associations or licensing boards that regulate entry into professions such as law, medicine, and teaching. In these fields, curriculum standards and learning outcomes are specified by leaders within the discipline or field of study. Academic program developers may need to address such standards and outcomes in their proposals for new programs.

Academic programs operate within a marketplace that includes potential students, employers of graduates, and competing programs at other institutions (Bok, 2003). Potential students are an important data source for academic program development. They can indicate preferences for curriculum delivery in terms of online, in-person, and hybrid formats. They can describe their intellectual and professional goals, which, in turn, can inform curriculum development. For existing programs, current students can provide data relevant to program growth and change. They can identify new subfields in which they want training and preparation and suggest additional support services that could assist with their academic success.

Employers constitute another source of data for academic program development. They can provide data directly to academic program developers through their participation on advisory boards that seek to ensure that the curriculum is relevant for the types of jobs that students are likely to obtain after graduation. Advisory board members can help faculty and staff understand how emerging trends in the field can inform teaching and learning practices. Academic program developers can also conduct employer surveys, where the results might identify the need to expand programs into new subfields or reform existing programs so that they incorporate new skills and content. To obtain a related perspective, program developers can survey alumni regarding how well a program of study prepared them for their profession. Some scholars, however, have questioned whether employers have too much influence over the curriculum. The emphasis on satisfying employers might contribute to student consumerism, in which higher education is viewed as simply another consumer good, rather than as an opportunity to pursue knowledge for its own sake (Molesworth, Nixon, & Scullion, 2009). To establish balance across multiple educational goals, academic program developers can consider how their proposals not only advance workforce development priorities but also contribute to the public good and the betterment of society as a whole (Rhoads & Szelényi, 2011).

Data regarding comparable programs at other institutions can also inform academic program development. Depending on the level of competition in the market, individuals at other institutions may or may not be willing to share data with academic program developers. However, a great deal of information is available through publicly accessible sources, such as institutional websites. Also, Integrated Postsecondary Education Data System (IPEDS) data can show the number of degrees that institutions award in a particular field (Posey & Pitter, 2012). If comparable programs at other institutions tend to award only a small number of degrees, then academic program developers can question whether a viable market exists for the proposed program, particularly if labor market projections are not suggesting future growth for the field. Information about comparable programs can also help program developers determine how they can position their proposed program as distinct from the competition. New programs may initially struggle to attract sufficient enrollments if they too closely resemble programs at other institutions that have been operating in the market for many years. Long-standing programs have reputations and resources that make them attractive to potential students, and thus provide a source of competitive advantage. Instead of competing head-to-head with long-standing programs, academic program developers can seek to identify a distinctive niche for their proposals. An analysis of comparable programs can reveal subfields and student populations that are not currently being served, and those areas could become the focal point for academic program development.

Although programs at other institutions are often viewed as competitors, they can also offer opportunities for collaboration. For example, academic programs at transfer institutions can be an important source of data for community college academic program development. Proposers of new academic programs at community colleges may need to demonstrate how the courses will transfer to programs of study at 4-year institutions. Thus, community college academic program developers may need to collaborate with faculty and staff at 4-year institutions, who can provide information regarding curricular design and desired learning outcomes for students who transfer into their programs of study. Similarly, graduate programs can provide important data to undergraduate programs, regarding the skills and knowledge bases that are needed for student success at the master's and doctoral levels. Undergraduate program developers could collect data from the graduate programs that accept the largest number of students from their institution.

Organizational Structure. Academic program developers can anticipate a range of structural issues that are likely to impact their efforts. High levels of structural differentiation and decentralization can complicate efforts to attract collaborators and obtain resources for program development. Academic program developers may also need to navigate through their institution's online and continuing education divisions, which often operate outside the structures of traditional academic departments. Furthermore, program development efforts often need to be aligned with institutional planning, budgeting, and governance structures that adhere to specific procedures, priorities, and time lines. Academic program developers may also need to assess the institution's structural capacity to support proposed program changes.

Most higher education institutions are structurally differentiated into a large number of academic departments. Given norms associated with academic freedom and professional autonomy, the faculty in these departments typically set their own curriculum and identify learning outcomes that are relevant to their respective disciplines. Although this structural arrangement aggregates the intellectual talents of faculty into coherent units, it also creates at least two challenges for academic program development. First, given that academic departments are the primary sites of academic program development, any effort that transcends these departmental boundaries may struggle to attract a sufficient number of collaborators (Kezar & Lester, 2009). Program development efforts that transcend departmental boundaries include general education reforms, first-year seminars, learning communities, service learning, and interdisciplinary initiatives. When faculty have extensive responsibilities in their own department, they may not have time for or may not develop an interest in collaborating on these types of institution-wide reforms. Second, the budget process at many institutions is based on credit hour production, which allocates funds to departments based on the number of students that they enroll. Enrollment-based budgeting, however, often serves as a disincentive for departments to collaborate on interdisciplinary initiatives. Under a system of enrollment-based budgeting, each unit will attempt to maximize its own enrollment, rather than explore opportunities to collaborate with other units on program development. Furthermore, given that enrollment-based budgeting directs the bulk of resources to academic departments, any initiative that exists outside the academic department structure might struggle to find the budgetary support that it needs (Keeling, Underhile, & Wall, 2007).

In addition to understanding the complexities of academic department structures, program developers may need to examine the policies and procedures of online and continuing education divisions. Many colleges and universities have developed online and continuing education divisions that seek to respond rapidly to emerging workforce development and professional preparation needs. These units tend to operate outside the typical academic department structure. Curricula may be developed by academic managers, rather than by faculty in academic departments (Toma, 2007). Decision-making processes are typically streamlined; new program proposals may not need to pass through multilevel approval processes that involve time-consuming deliberations by governance committees. The funding model for these units is often designed to generate revenue. This goal can be pursued by employing part-time faculty and/or by charging differential tuition rates. By generating surplus revenues, these units can operate at least somewhat independently from the institution's budget process. With their own funding streams secure, they can pursue new ventures without being overly concerned if some new programs initially fail to generate sufficient enrollments. In summary, the policies and procedures of online and continuing education divisions are likely to be quite different from those that govern academic departments. If academic program developers will be collaborating with these online and continuing education units, then they will need to become familiar with a different business model and a different mind-set for academic decision making.

Beyond the academic departments and divisions that comprise a college or university are institution-wide planning, budgeting, and governance committees that seek to advance the interests of the organization as a whole. Proposals for new programs or initiatives to expand or modify existing programs often need to be approved by faculty governance committees, as well as by planning and budgeting committees that are comprised mostly of administrators (Bess & Dee, 2008). Academic program developers can tailor their presentations of data to the expectations and preferences of the various parties involved in these processes. Faculty committee members, for example, might expect to see data that relate to the academic quality of the proposed curriculum, the qualifications of the faculty who will teach in the new or modified program, and the resources that will be available to support student success, such as advising, library materials, and instructional technology. Administrators might expect to see data that focus on projected enrollments, revenues, and expenses. They might also expect that the proposed program will be linked to themes and priorities expressed in the institution's strategic plan. Connecting academic program proposals to the strategic plan is important, because at many institutions, administrators allocate resources based on the extent to which a proposed initiative can contribute to the institution's strategic priorities. Academic program developers can use data to make a compelling case that the proposed or modified program will advance institutional goals and priorities.

Before academic program developers can fulfill the data expectations of various committee members, they might need to assess the institution's structural capacity for implementing the academic changes they are proposing. Program developers may be required to provide detailed information on the resources that will be needed to implement the new program or modify an existing program (Posey & Pitter, 2012). Institutions may require that such proposals differentiate between resources that are currently available, and new resources that will need to be acquired or reallocated. In such cases, program developers will need to assess the capacity of existing structures to support their proposal. Structural needs for program development include the availability of faculty, classroom and laboratory facilities, library and instructional technology resources, student advising and support services, and faculty development and training. In addition to considering the infrastructure needed to implement a proposed program, academic program developers can also assess the institution's capacity for collecting and analyzing data to support academic proposal development. Large institutions may have sizable institutional research offices in which particular staff members have been assigned responsibility to support academic program development. In this context, institutional research offices may routinely collect program-level data that track student performance, measure student engagement and satisfaction, and monitor retention and graduation rates. In smaller institutions, capacities for data collection and analysis may be more limited. In some cases, outside consultants or market research firms may be hired to provide data and analysis in areas for which the institution does not have sufficient expertise.

Organizational Culture. Although a consideration of external environments and organizational structures can provide an understanding of the key stakeholders and venues in which decision making occurs, an analysis of organizational culture offers insights into the values and beliefs that shape those decisions. Most conceptualizations of organizational culture suggest that it comprised a set of values and beliefs that are widely shared in an organization and that guide decisions and actions (Schein, 1992). The organizational cultures of most colleges and universities, however, seldom present a unified set of values and beliefs. Instead, higher education institutions are characterized by multiple, and sometimes conflicting, subcultures (Bess & Dee, 2014). The subcultural differences that are most likely to affect academic program development include the divide between faculty and administrative subcultures, as well as the subcultural differences among faculty themselves, based on distinct traditions in the disciplines in which they have been trained. The tensions among subcultures are not necessarily dysfunctional. Higher education institutions have historically embraced divergent values and beliefs so that creative thinking can emerge and new knowledge can be produced. Most organizational members in higher education institutions will adhere strongly to their respective subcultural values. Thus, rather than try to get different subcultures to unite around common values, academic program developers can frame proposed changes in ways that connect to multiple value systems.

Given that proposals for new programs and changes to existing programs often need to be approved by committees comprised of faculty and administrators, academic program developers must learn to work with both subcultures. In broad terms, the administrative subculture values consistency and efficiency, whereas the faculty subculture values freedom and flexibility (Kezar, 2014). These differences in values often lead to tensions between administrators, who seek to centralize and standardize practices (to promote efficiency and coordination), and faculty, who prefer decentralization and customized approaches (to preserve freedom of thought and action). An examination of these subcultures can also reveal differences in beliefs about data. In the context of significant pressures to demonstrate accountability, administrators might view data as a tool to measure effectiveness and efficiency. Faculty, in contrast, might be more skeptical about institutional data. They might be concerned that data will be used punitively. For example, if student learning outcomes data show a decline in performance, then faculty may worry that administrators will blame them for the problem, rather than provide more resources to support student success.

A further difference between the administrative and faculty subcultures pertains to their motivation for academic program development. Faculty are motivated to engage in program development because they want to explore emerging trends within their disciplines and fields of study (Clark, 1996). If a new domain of knowledge becomes relevant within their discipline, then faculty may want to develop new courses or programs of study in that area. In contrast, administrators are motivated to engage in program development because such efforts can generate revenues and enhance the prestige and reputation of the institution. Although these motivations are not inherently contradictory, some scholars have questioned whether so many academic decisions should be guided by a revenue-generation logic (Slaughter & Rhoades, 2004). The focus on revenue generation might displace other historically valued goals of higher education, including initiatives that seek to advance the public good (Rhoads & Szelényi, 2011), as well as efforts to enhance programs in disciplines that are far removed from the market, such as the arts and humanities.

Although understanding the differences between administrative and faculty subcultures is important to successful academic program development, program developers can also consider the subcultural differences among faculty. Given the different ontological and epistemological assumptions that characterize the various disciplines, faculty are likely to have quite different views regarding what constitutes effective teaching and what counts as valid research (Becher & Trowler, 2001). In terms of academic decision making, faculty may use their disciplinary research assumptions to assess the quality and validity of institutional data. If faculty are accustomed to using experimental designs with control groups in their own research, then they might view academic program proposals as lacking rigor if they contain only descriptive statistics and frequency counts. In contrast, if faculty work in disciplines that primarily use qualitative methods, then they might question whether statistical reports can capture underlying meanings and unique experiences of people and groups. Furthermore, some departmental subcultures have a longer history of data-based decision making. Professional fields with accreditation, for example, have engaged in student outcomes assessment for many years. Their knowledge and familiarity with institutional data will likely be greater than departments with less engagement in assessment (Dill, 1999). Academic program developers will need to be sensitive to these disciplinary differences, particularly in two scenarios:

> When a proposal for program development emerges in one department, but will be evaluated by faculty committee members from other departments
>
> When a proposal for program development pertains to an institution-wide initiative, such as first-year seminars or general education, that will involve faculty from multiple disciplines

Although colleges and universities are fragmented into multiple subcultures, these institutions also have some overarching values and beliefs that characterize the organization as a whole, and which may affect academic program development. Birnbaum (1988) suggests that although colleges and universities have multiple sets of values and beliefs, each institution is characterized by a particular cultural model, such as collegial or bureaucratic. Research has shown that change processes, including academic program development, are more likely to be successful if organizational members align their strategies for change with the cultural values of their institution (Kezar & Eckel, 2002). For example, if the culture at an institution is primarily bureaucratic, then change agents might be more successful if they engage with formal committees and follow a clear chain of command. Specific dimensions of the organizational culture can also affect academic program development. The degree to which risk taking and innovation are valued in the organizational culture, for example, can signal whether new academic initiatives will be met with resistance or enthusiasm.

Organizational Power. The ability of organizational members to achieve outcomes that reflect their values depends, in large part, on the amount of power that they hold in the organization. In fact, the success of an academic program proposal depends not only on the quality of the data but also on the power possessed by the person or group presenting the proposal. Organizational power is derived from a variety of sources, including the formal authority associated with a hierarchical position such as dean or provost, as well as informal sources of power that emerge through social networks and interpersonal connections (Yukl, 2002). When viewed in terms of power dynamics, academic program development entails competition, negotiation, and bargaining, and requires political skills such as alliance building.

Power dynamics in colleges and universities emerge, in part, from the multiple and broadly framed goals of higher education. As noted earlier in this chapter, the goals of teaching, research, and service are somewhat vague, difficult to measure, and subject to multiple interpretations. These ambiguous goals do not provide an objective basis for academic decision making. Data-based arguments may not persuade organizational members who interpret the institution's goals in different ways. Instead, negotiating, bargaining, and alliance building may be necessary to advance proposals for change. As Temple (2008) notes, an academic decision is often deemed successful not because it fulfills some rational objective standard, but because it attracts sufficient political support from key groups within the organization.

The shared governance committees described earlier in this chapter often become venues for political conflict between faculty and administrators. The norms of shared governance suggest that decisions regarding curriculum, teaching, and learning should be delegated to faculty governance committees, whereas decisions that involve budgets and institutional strategy should be determined by administrators who seek advice on those decisions from the faculty. Although this statement appears to clarify the shared governance roles of faculty and administrators, in practice, the boundary between these domains is not entirely clear. The curricular decisions of faculty are likely to have budgetary implications, and the budget decisions of administrators may limit the types of curricular decisions that faculty can make. Thus, when decisions involve curriculum, budgets, and strategy, some degree of conflict is likely to emerge between administrators and faculty.

The institutional budget-setting process is a particularly intense arena for conflict. As noted previously, some institutions allocate resources on the basis of enrollment. Departments that enroll more students receive a larger share of institutional funds. Although this arrangement serves as an incentive for program growth, it also pits departments against each other for funding. Milam and Brinkman (2012) note that "the addition of enrollments to an existing major or the creation of new majors or a program may have a significant impact on departments other than the one responsible for the major's home" (p. 215). Department chairs and faculty may see academic program development as a zero-sum game, in which enrollment and resource gains for new programs in other departments come at the expense of enrollments and resources for their department.

The power dynamics of program development become even more complicated in multicampus systems, where other institutions in the system may be able to veto proposals for programs that they believe would compete with their degree offerings. Nearly all institutions offer programs in the basic arts and sciences disciplines that provide the core undergraduate curriculum. Beyond those disciplines, the mix of academic programs offered by a particular institution may depend on the domains already occupied by other public higher education institutions in the state. If a flagship university has already established a school of engineering, for example, then another university in that same state system might be blocked from pursuing a similar initiative. The extent to which a new program at one institution competes with existing programs at other system institutions is, however, often a subjective matter. An institution might seek to develop a new program that occupies a unique niche in a particular field, but another university in the same state system might discount the unique aspects of the program, and instead see the proposal as a threat to their own enrollments and revenue.

The Decision Context

Along with the general context of the organization, the specific context of the decision shapes how the decision-making process will unfold. Important components of the decision context include the type and scope of the decision being considered, the organization's history with similar decisions, and the current stage of the decision-making process. These components can influence whether internal or external data are emphasized, and whether organizational members engage in objective or subjective analyses of those data.

Three types of decisions characterize academic program development: the creation of a new program, the expansion of an existing program, or the substantial modification of an existing program. If the decision pertains to the expansion or modification of an existing program, then organizational members will focus primarily on internal data. Academic program developers may need to gather and analyze data regarding student performance and outcomes in the existing program (Posey & Pitter, 2012). If student performance and outcomes are problematic, then expansion of the program may not be warranted until the existing program is improved. In addition, previous program reviews or accreditation reports can be examined to identify strengths and areas for improvement, which, in turn, can serve as the basis for program expansion or modification (Bogue & Saunders, 1992). Although the focus will be directed mostly toward internal data, some external data might be needed to document trends in the discipline if the program is expanding into new subfields, or trends in professional practice if the program is modifying its curriculum to include new competencies to prepare students for employment more thoroughly.

In contrast to the internal data focus for expanding or modifying an existing program, new program development will rely primarily on external data. Program developers will need to consider data on the enrollment market for students and the labor market for graduates in the proposed program area. Data from government agencies, businesses, and industry groups might be needed if the new program is intended to fulfill workforce development needs in the state or region. Although the data focus for new program development will be mostly external, some internal data might be needed to assess the extent to which the institution can support the new program in areas such as faculty resources and facilities.

The scope of the decision will also affect the use of data. The scope of a program development decision may be institution-wide, such as a change in the general education curriculum, or specific to a particular department or program. If the scope of the decision is institution-wide, then data analysis is likely to be more subjective and political. An institution-wide proposal might compel academic departments to change at least some of their courses, teaching practices, or academic policies. Such changes might provoke resistance from faculty and administrators who were not involved in developing the proposal (Esterberg & Wooding, 2012). Furthermore, the various academic departments are likely to have different interpretations of institutional goals and priorities, and their members might prefer that the institution pursue other initiatives, rather than what has been proposed. In contrast, if the scope of the decision relates only to a particular program or department, then data analysis might be more objective. Faculty and administrators in other departments might defer to the expertise and judgment of their colleagues in the department that has proposed the change. If the proposed change will have minimal impact on other departments, then organizational members will likely not challenge or question how the proposing department has analyzed and interpreted supporting data. However, if the department's proposal is seen as having major resource implications, then other departments might view the proposal in terms of a zero-sum competition for resources (Milam & Brinkman, 2012), and the analysis of data then becomes more subjective and political.

The institution's history with similar decisions also shapes the decision-making process. If the institution has made similar decisions in the past, and will likely continue to make such decisions in the future, then institutional leaders may create standard procedures for making these routine decisions (Huber & McDaniel, 1986). For example, a community college that creates a large number of workforce development programs may have standard procedures for interacting with local businesses, collecting relevant data, and creating new program proposals. When routine decision-making processes are used, data analysis is likely to be more objective, because agreed-upon criteria for decision making have already been established. In contrast, when the institution has made few or no decisions in a particular domain, data analysis is likely to be more subjective. If the content is unfamiliar to organizational members, then they might not know how to interpret the proposal. Here, multiple and potentially conflicting interpretations of the proposal may emerge, thus leading to a subjective analysis of data.

Finally, data usage will differ depending on the stage of the decision-making process (Mintzberg et al., 1976). At early stages, decision makers might use data to identify or understand a problem. In this scenario, data analysis would likely be subjective, because the specific problem has not been identified yet or is still open to interpretation. At middle stages, decision makers may want data that help them select among several alternative courses of action. Here, data analysis would be somewhat objective, because the problem has now been defined and options for addressing the problem have been identified. For example, a department might discover that it has a problem with student retention. Department members could then examine student outcomes data and determine if students tend to depart at certain times during their program of study, or if performance in a particular course is associated with whether students persist in the major. Such analyses can suggest which alternative courses of action—enhanced advising, new teaching practices, or curricular changes—could improve retention rates. Finally, at later stages, data might be used to determine how best to implement a chosen course of action. At this stage, data analysis would likely be objective, because a course of action has already been selected. For example, if a department has decided to implement first-year seminars to improve retention, faculty members may want data from other departments that have used this practice to determine if the seminars should be co-taught and/or paired with another required course.

Four Decision Models

The organizational context (environment, structure, culture, and power dynamics) and the decision context (type, scope, history, and stage of decision) influence how data will be used in decisions regarding academic program development. Specifically, these contextual variables shape the relative importance of internal and external data in the decision-making process. These variables can also suggest whether data are likely to be analyzed objectively or subjectively. When considered together, these two dimensions (internal/external and objective/subjective) yield four decision models: rational, entrepreneurial, political, and exploratory. This section of the chapter provides a brief explanation of each model. In addition, the four models are illustrated with examples from a case study of online program development at three community colleges. We refer to these colleges using pseudonyms.

Rational Model. The rational model is based on research that examines managerial decision making. Researchers in this tradition suggest that decisions are more likely to enhance organizational effectiveness when managers follow a linear process that involves data collection and analysis (Dean & Sharfman, 1993; Fredrickson, 1984; March & Simon, 1958). The process typically begins with gathering and analyzing data on organizational performance. When performance is less than optimal, managers attempt to identify or diagnose the problems that might be interfering with the organization's capacity to achieve its goals. After a problem has been identified, managers will consider a range of options to address the problem, as well as identify the criteria they will use to select among those options. At this point in the process, managers can gather additional information about the feasibility and likely success of the various options they are considering. After managers select a particular course of action, they will allocate resources and direct personnel to implement the decision, as well as establish feedback mechanisms to gauge how well the decision addresses the problem. This model assumes that data, analyzed objectively, will lead to choices that maximize the effectiveness of the organization.

The rational model depicts an ideal decision-making scenario in which people have all of the relevant information they need to make a decision, as well as sufficient time to analyze that information. Such favorable conditions, however, are unlikely to materialize for many decisions. Data might be unavailable, irrelevant to the problem, or overwhelming in volume and complexity. Even if the right data are available, people may lack the time or expertise to interpret them. Under these more typical conditions, organizational members tend to consider just a few options that differ only slightly from the status quo. This simplified process enables people to address more quickly a larger number of organizational problems. But the problematic implication is that decision makers are not considering more innovative approaches to addressing organizational problems, and thus, the decisions that they make may have only a marginal impact on improving organizational outcomes. This simplified process, which Lindblom (1959) described as "muddling through," suggests that organizational members attempt to make rational decisions, but they encounter shortcomings in their capacity to enact fully each step in the process. For the purpose of this chapter, we consider the rational model to include processes in which decision makers thoroughly gather and analyze data on a wide range of options, as well as instances in which only a simplified version of the model is carried out.

In the context of academic program development, the rational model draws attention to internal data about institutional performance and outcomes. Data on retention, degree completion, or student learning outcomes, for example, could reveal problems that need to be addressed at the level of specific academic programs or the institution as a whole. Although the focus is on internal data, decision makers are not necessarily neglecting external considerations, because accountability pressures from external stakeholders have been a strong driving force for the collection of internal data on institutional performance. The rational model also assumes that the parties involved in academic program development will analyze internal data objectively. Objective analysis usually depends on the parties having some sort of common understanding of the problem, as well as agreement on the criteria that will be used to select a course of action to address the problem.

Example of a Rational Decision. Decision makers at Zorn Valley Community College enacted a rational model to select a new learning management system (LMS) for online courses. Administrators detected a problem with the college's existing LMS when they examined internal data provided by faculty and students. "There were a lot of complaints about it," noted one administrator. "We had some irate, unhappy faculty who were threatening to no longer use [the college's LMS], and we were going to lose them [from the online program]." A staff member in the academic technology office reported that "students were yelling that it [the LMS] wasn't working with the version of the browser they were using." The provost decided that the issue constituted a threat to the quality of online education at the college, and therefore asked the Academic Technology Committee to investigate options for change.

The Academic Technology Committee created a separate subcommittee to explore LMS alternatives. The subcommittee had broad representation from faculty, technology staff, and academic administration. An administrator noted that the decision process "was very collegial, collaborative; everyone felt they played a role in it and had some input." The subcommittee identified six LMS options. After reviewing information provided by vendors and after speaking with colleagues at other colleges who were using a variety of systems, the committee narrowed its choice to three alternatives.

Each of the three LMS finalists was then piloted in two separate online courses. These live pilots allowed data to be gathered from six experienced online instructors and their students. The piloting faculty members filled out detailed questionnaires and used a common rubric to rate their LMS. An administrator noted that the rubric provided specific data about each component of the LMS: "they took one piece, such as grading. Then, two faculty looked at grading in each of the systems. It was a really thorough process." Although the subcommittee used some external data from vendors and other colleges, the focus was primarily on internal data provided by students and faculty. The parties involved in the process—administrators, technology staff, and faculty—had a similar understanding of the problem, and they developed an objective rubric for selecting an LMS from the options they were considering.

Entrepreneurial Model. As with the rational model, the entrepreneurial model assumes that data will be analyzed objectively, but the focus shifts to external data sources. The entrepreneurial model becomes relevant when organizational members perceive an opportunity in the external environment (Clark, 1998; Keller, 1983). The opportunity might be a new student market or an emerging academic subfield that has potential for growth. Organizational members may then collect data from the external environment to confirm that the opportunity actually exists, and to determine whether the institution should pursue that opportunity. To make these assessments, decision makers would likely collect data on projected enrollments, labor market demand for graduates, and instructional trends within the discipline or field of study. They might also consult external stakeholders, such as government policy makers and employers, particularly if the opportunity relates to addressing workforce development needs. Finally, if organizational members decide to pursue a particular opportunity, they could collect additional data regarding how best to implement their decision. Here, academic program developers could consider how other institutions have designed and implemented similar programs.

Huber (1991) has described this type of external data collection as focused search. When organizational members engage in focused search, they seek to acquire information about a specific opportunity that they want to pursue. Focused search depends on having organizational members who are willing to innovate and take risks with new ideas that they observe in the external environment. The potential downside of focused search is that organizational members may become so committed to pursuing an identified opportunity that they no longer objectively analyze the external data. They might discount indicators of weak student demand, for instance, and push forward with developing a new program anyway.

The entrepreneurial model assumes that organizational members have set clear goals and priorities to guide their engagement with the external environment (Alfred, 2001). Given limited resources, organizations cannot pursue every opportunity that emerges in the external environment. Goals and priorities help organizational members decide which opportunities to pursue. In higher education institutions, these goals and priorities are often expressed in strategic plans. These plans might include specific strategies for academic program growth and development. An objective analysis of external data could help organizational members determine how best to implement these strategic initiatives.

Example of an Entrepreneurial Decision. Administrators and faculty at Wilder Community College decided to put an allied health program online. The existing on-campus program consistently drew large enrollments, and given limited resources for new facilities, the online environment was viewed as the best way to expand the program. As a faculty member explained, "it is sort of like 'if you build it, they will come.' Every community college in the state has a problem with way more qualified applicants than available spaces [for this type of health program]." Others explained the idea as a way to advance the college's strategic goal of putting as many courses and programs online as possible, in order to expand access and stabilize institutional revenues. Both administrators and faculty expressed excitement about being the first college in the state to have such a health program online.

The novelty of the proposal, however, meant that faculty and administrators at Wilder were unsure about how best to put this program online. They recognized that they needed to gather more data. Administrators granted a sabbatical to a faculty member in the existing on-campus program. The sabbatical allowed the faculty member to collect data on similar programs in other states. The faculty member found that most of these programs were at the 4-year or graduate level. In fact, only one community college program was identified. "We invited a faculty member from that [community college] program to come here and meet with us," recalled an administrator. "She gave us some pointers." The primary lesson that came from studying other programs was the value of students demonstrating their comprehension of course learning outcomes through online discussion boards. This approach was incorporated into the courses developed for the Wilder online health program.

Political Model. Although the rational and entrepreneurial models depend on objective data analysis, the political model is characterized by subjective analysis. The model notes that many individuals and groups are involved in organizational decision making, and the values, interests, and goals of these individuals and groups will often conflict and produce different interpretations of the same data (Allison, 1971; Pfeffer & Salancik, 1974). According to the political model, decisions are the product of bargaining and competition among organizational members who have varying degrees of power. Data and information are tools in a competition for power, rather than evidence to help make an objective judgment. Organizational members may look only for information that supports their own position or that undermines the position of their adversaries. Once they obtain information, they may hide, manipulate, or release it selectively to influence decisions.

The political model assumes that multiple individuals and groups are involved in the decision-making process because no single individual has the power, expertise, or information to make decisions alone. Those assumptions also guide the practices of shared governance, in which many actors play a role in institutional decisions. Governance committees, in fact, can be viewed as venues in which the political interests of various groups are expressed and negotiated (Baldridge, 1971). Although the involvement of actors from different parts of an institution could lead to dysfunctional conflict, it could also be the basis for cooperation, including the sharing of data and the incorporation of multiple points of view in the interpretation of those data. In some cases, political behavior can actually improve decisions (Rahim, 2002). Organizational politics can alert decision makers to sources of opposition that could be detrimental to the implementation of the decision. Political behavior also compels decision makers to consider a range of viewpoints, which may lead to a reframing of the problem or to the consideration of new alternatives. This model also allows organizational members to express their voices and feel involved in the process, even if the final decision does not reflect their views.

Example of a Political Decision. A decision about whether to continue to offer two biology courses online at Yankee Community College followed a political model. The Dean of Continuing Education at Yankee made regular announcements to all faculty asking if they wished to put classes online. None of the full-time biology professors expressed an interest; however, an adjunct instructor agreed to move two existing biology classes with lab components into an online format. The lab portion of these two courses included a variety of simulations and virtual tools that attempted to replicate the experience of a hands-on lab. These two courses ran this way for nearly 5 years without issue. Eventually, however, full-time biology faculty began to raise questions about these courses. They asked why the courses had not been developed by a full-time professor. More fundamentally, they challenged the idea that the student experience in the lab could be successfully simulated online. An administrator noted that "the biologists have taken the position that the lab is the lab, and if you are not [physically] in a lab, then you're not in a lab." Hands-on experience in the lab was viewed as crucial by these faculty members. As a full-time professor argued, "there is that tactile aspect to science where students should be handling the equipment and the different tools."

The Dean worked to allay these concerns. The full-time faculty were invited to look at the online course materials and also to view demonstrations of the types of laboratory simulations that were available online so that they could see their sophistication and quality. Furthermore, the Dean gathered data on the success of the students who had taken the online lab courses. As another administrator indicated, the data showed that "the course completion was fine. . . Students who took [the] online course went on to other courses and were just as successful; so there was no divergence in the grades."

These data did not assuage the full-time biology faculty. "The data did exist for that, but it did not matter," said one full-time instructor. The issue was one of principle and did not hang on course completion rates as far as the full-time biology professors were concerned. An administrator remarked that "the biology department has taken a firm theological position that you cannot teach a lab science online, period, end of conversation, thank you very much."

Given the intensity of this opposition and the authority of the Dean of Continuing Education to keep the courses online, the full-time biology faculty chose to take the issue to the college senate. The full-time biology professors brought forward a motion demanding that science classes with labs must have approval from their respective academic department before they can be offered online. An administrator described the senate meeting at which the vote was taken. "The person [from the biology department] got up and gave an impassioned plea, and they [senate members] bought it." The biology professors' motion passed by a large margin.

The impact of this decision was substantial. Existing online science courses with labs now had to go through the curriculum approval process, the first step of which was department review. As the biology department approved of neither of the two online biology lab courses, these courses were forced out of the online program. Students who needed a biology course for their program of study found that they could no longer complete their requirements online. According to a frustrated administrator, "it is really creating an issue for us, because it is preventing us from doing some complete degree programs [online]."

Exploratory Model. The exploratory model describes a scenario in which organizational members are engaged in subjective analyses of external data. Although both the exploratory model and the entrepreneurial model focus on external data, the two models are characterized by some important differences. In the entrepreneurial model, decision makers have already identified an opportunity in the external environment, and they have decided to conduct a focused search for more information about the feasibility of pursuing that opportunity. In contrast, the exploratory model is enacted through a general scanning of the environment. This type of general scan is conducted not to explore a particular opportunity, but rather to gather information about external trends and emerging practices in the field. Exploratory data analysis is subjective because, in these cases, organizational members have not identified a particular problem to solve or established an agreed-upon course of action, in contrast to the entrepreneurial model, which presumes consensus about how to move forward with an identified opportunity. According to March (1991), there is an interactive relationship between the entrepreneurial and exploratory models. A general exploration of the environment is likely to identify specific opportunities that could be exploited through entrepreneurial decisions and actions.

The exploratory model may be particularly relevant during periods of uncertainty (Mintzberg, 1990). The other three models describe scenarios in which people have some degree of certainty and clarity. In the rational model, decision makers are focused on a particular problem to solve.

The entrepreneurial model focuses on a specific opportunity to exploit. The political model focuses on a particular conflict to adjudicate or negotiate. In contrast, the exploratory model assumes that organizational members are unsure about how to proceed, but they are willing to embrace uncertainty as an opportunity to learn. In academic program development, the exploratory model can describe the behaviors of faculty, staff, and administrators who seek to prepare themselves for making effective decisions about program growth and development. When they lack certainty about how to proceed, academic program developers can seek external data by attending conferences, participating in consortiums, and studying what other institutions are doing.

Example of an Exploratory Decision. A general concern for quality motivated online program developers at Wilder Community College to engage frequently in environmental scanning. An administrator noted that "because distance learning is still somewhat new for a lot of people, it probably gets more scrutiny than other programs. We have to make sure that we are up to speed on what's going on in the field." Faculty and administrators frequently attended conferences about online learning, and they stayed in touch with colleagues at other institutions who were involved in online programs in similar fields.

Furthermore, Wilder Community College was an active member in a statewide consortium on online education, and the institution had established an informal partnership with one of the state universities. As an administrator explained, the partnership involved training and professional development. "They [faculty and administrators at the state university] gave us all kinds of information, [and they] came down and did seminars for our faculty to get them up to speed in the online environment." This administrator also noted that the partnership helped Wilder Community College deal with the uncertainties associated with developing new online programs. "At the time, [the partnership] was sort of our insurance policy that getting into this, we were at least going to get into it successfully. We were not going to make all the mistakes they [the state university] made; they made sure of that and they mentored us."

When Wilder Community College needed to select a new hosting solution for its online course delivery, rather than engage in a detailed rational analysis, as Zorn Valley did to select a new LMS, decision makers instead turned to their state university partner. They selected the state university as the venue to provide the servers to host Wilder's online courses. An administrator explained that the decision "seemed like a no-brainer."

Conclusion

When academic program developers understand the context of the organization and the context of the decision that they are pursuing, they will be better able to anticipate which decision-making model is likely to emerge

Table 1.1. Influence of Selected Contextual Variables on the Decision Process

Model Likely to Emerge	*Organizational Context*	*Decision Context*
Rational model	E: stable S: centralized C: bureaucratic P: common interests	Type: existing program Scope: single department History: familiar Stage: later
Entrepreneurial model	E: dynamic S: centralized C: risk-taking, innovative P: common interests	Type: new program Scope: single department History: familiar Stage: later
Political model	E: stable S: decentralized, multilayered C: bureaucratic P: divergent interests	Type: existing program Scope: institution-wide History: unfamiliar Stage: early
Exploratory model	E: dynamic S: decentralized, multilayered C: risk-taking, innovative P: divergent interests	Type: new program Scope: institution-wide History: unfamiliar Stage: early

Note: E = environment, S = structure, C = culture, P = power dynamics.

(rational, entrepreneurial, political, or exploratory). Data are used and interpreted in different ways based on the model that emerges. If academic program developers can anticipate which model will emerge, then they will be better prepared to address the data needs and expectations of key stakeholders in the decision. For example, if the rational model is likely to emerge, then they can gather and distribute internal data and assist in an objective analysis of those data. If the political model is likely to emerge instead, they can consider how the various stakeholder groups will interpret internal data in different ways. If the entrepreneurial model is anticipated, then program developers can focus on external data and facilitate an objective appraisal of environmental conditions. If the exploratory model is expected, then program developers can engage their professional networks and bring external data into the institution, where it will be interpreted in a variety of ways.

Table 1.1 indicates how some contextual variables can affect which decision-making model is likely to emerge. The table does not provide a complete listing of all possible variables, but it can help program developers make an initial assessment of the context and thereby anticipate which decision-making model they are likely to encounter. Furthermore, the process for a particular decision may shift from one model to another. Program developers can continue to monitor the organizational and decision contexts throughout the decision-making process, and thus prepare themselves for these types of changes.

References

Alfred, R. (2001). Strategic thinking: The untapped resource for leaders. *Community College Journal, 71*(3), 24–28.
Allison, G. (1971). *Essence of decision: Explaining the Cuban missile crisis*. Boston, MA: Little, Brown.
Baldridge, J. (1971). *Power and conflict in the university*. New York, NY: John Wiley.
Becher, T., & Trowler, P. R. (2001). *Academic tribes and territories: Intellectual inquiry and the culture of disciplines* (2nd ed.). Buckingham, United Kingdom: Open University Press/Society for Research into Higher Education.
Bess, J., & Dee, J. (2008). *Understanding college and university organization: Theories for effective policy and practice* (Vols. 1 and 2). Sterling, VA: Stylus Publishing.
Bess, J., & Dee, J. (2014). *Bridging the divide between faculty and administration: A guide to understanding conflict in the academy*. New York, NY: Routledge.
Birnbaum, R. (1988). *How colleges work: The cybernetics of academic organization and leadership*. San Francisco, CA: Jossey-Bass.
Bogue, E., & Saunders, R. (1992). *The evidence for quality: Strengthening the tests of academic and administrative effectiveness*. San Francisco, CA: Jossey-Bass.
Bok, D. (2003). *Universities in the marketplace: The commercialization of higher education*. Princeton, NJ: Princeton University Press.
Clark, B. (1983). *The higher education system: Academic organization in cross-national perspective*. Berkeley: University of California Press.
Clark, B. (1996). Substantive growth and innovative organization: New categories for higher education research. *Higher Education, 32*, 417–430.
Clark, B. (1998). *Creating entrepreneurial universities: Organizational pathways of transformation*. New York, NY: Pergamon.
Dean, J., & Sharfman, M. (1993). Procedural rationality in the strategic decision-making process. *Journal of Management Studies, 30*, 587–610.
Dill, D. (1999). Academic accountability and university adaptation: The architecture of an academic learning organization. *Higher Education, 38*, 127–154.
Elbanna, S., & Child, J. (2007). The influence of decision, environmental, and firm characteristics on the rationality of strategic decision-making. *Journal of Management Studies, 44*(4), 561–591.
Esterberg, K. G., & Wooding, J. (2012). *Divided conversations: Identities, leadership, and change in public higher education*. Nashville, TN: Vanderbilt University Press.
Fredrickson, J. (1984). The comprehensiveness of strategic decision processes: Extension, observations, future directions. *Academy of Management Journal, 27*, 445–466.
Heineman, W. (2011). *The role of data in decision making about online distance education: A case study of three community colleges* (Unpublished doctoral dissertation). University of Massachusetts, Boston.
Huber, G. (1991). Organizational learning: The contributing processes and the literatures. *Organization Science, 2*(1), 88–115.
Huber, G., & McDaniel, R. (1986). The decision-making paradigm of organizational design. *Management Science, 32*(5), 572–589.
Keeling, R., Underhile, R., & Wall, A. (2007). Horizontal and vertical structures: The dynamics of organization in higher education. *Liberal Education, 93*(4), 22–31.
Keller, G. (1983). *Academic strategy: The management revolution in higher education*. Baltimore, MD: Johns Hopkins University Press.
Kezar, A. (2014). *How colleges change: Understanding, leading, and enacting change*. New York, NY: Routledge.
Kezar, A., & Eckel, P. (2002). The effects of institutional culture on change strategies in higher education: Universal principles or culturally responsive concepts. *Journal of Higher Education, 73*(4), 443–460.

Kezar, A., & Lester, J. (2009). *Organizing higher education for collaboration: A guide for campus leaders*. San Francisco: Jossey-Bass.

Lindblom, C. (1959). The science of muddling through. *Public Administration Review*, *19*, 79–88.

March, J. (1991). Exploration and exploitation in organizational learning. *Organization Science*, *2*, 71–87.

March, J., & Simon, H. (1958). *Organizations*. New York, NY: John Wiley.

Milam, J., & Brinkman, P. (2012). Building cost models. In R. Howard, G. McLaughlin, & W. Knight (Eds.), *The handbook of institutional research* (pp. 203–220). San Francisco, CA: Jossey-Bass.

Mintzberg, H. (1990). The design school: Reconsidering the basic premises of strategic management. *Strategic Management Journal*, *11*(3), 171–195.

Mintzberg, H., Raisinghani, D., & Theoret, A. (1976). The structure of "unstructured" decision processes. *Administrative Science Quarterly*, *21*, 246–275.

Molesworth, M., Nixon, E., & Scullion, R. (2009). Having, being, and higher education: The marketization of the university and the transformation of the student into consumer. *Teaching in Higher Education*, *14*(3), 277–287.

Morphew, C., & Hartley, M. (2006). Mission statements: A thematic analysis of rhetoric across institutional type. *Journal of Higher Education*, *77*(3), 456–471.

Papadakis, V., Lioukas, S., & Chambers, D. (1998). Strategic decision-making processes: The role of management and context. *Strategic Management Journal*, *19*, 115–147.

Pfeffer, J., & Salancik, G. (1974). Organizational decision making as a political process: The case of a university budget. *Administrative Science Quarterly*, *19*, 135–151.

Posey, J., & Pitter, G. W. (2012). Supporting the provost and academic vice president. In R. Howard, G. McLaughlin, & W. Knight (Eds.), *The handbook of institutional research* (pp. 145–164). San Francisco, CA: Jossey-Bass.

Rahim, M. (2002). Toward a theory of managing organizational conflict. *International Journal of Conflict Management*, *13*(3), 206–235.

Rhoads, R., & Szelényi, K. (2011). *Global citizenship and the university: Advancing social life and relations in an interdependent world*. Stanford, CA: Stanford University Press.

Schein, E. (1992). *Organizational culture and leadership* (2nd ed.). San Francisco, CA: Jossey-Bass.

Schmidtlein, F. (1999). Common assumptions about organizations that mislead institutional researchers and their clients. *Research in Higher Education*, *40*(5), 571–587.

Shepherd, N., & Rudd, J. (2014). The influence of context on the strategic decision-making process: A review of the literature. *International Journal of Management Reviews*, *16*, 340–364.

Slaughter, S., & Rhoades, G. (2004). *Academic capitalism and the new economy: Markets, state, and higher education*. Baltimore, MD: Johns Hopkins University Press.

Tarter, J., & Hoy, W. (1998). Toward a contingency theory of decision making. *Journal of Educational Administration*, *36*(3), 212–228.

Temple, P. (2008). The integrative university. *Perspectives: Policy and Practice in Higher Education*, *12*(4), 99–102.

Terenzini, P. (1993). On the nature of institutional research and the knowledge and skills it requires. *Research in Higher Education*, *34*(1), 1–10.

Tierney, W. (2001). Why committees don't work: Creating a structure for change. *Academe*, *87*(3), 25–29.

Toma, J. D. (2007). Expanding peripheral activities, increasing accountability demands, and reconsidering governance in U.S. higher education. *Higher Education Research and Development*, *26*(1), 57–72.

Wellman, J. (2006). Rethinking state governance of higher education. In W. Tierney (Ed.), *Governance and the public good* (pp. 51–72). Albany, NY: State University of New York Press.
Yukl, G. (2002). *Leadership in organizations* (5th ed.). Upper Saddle River, NJ: Prentice Hall.

JAY R. DEE is associate professor and director of the Higher Education program at the University of Massachusetts, Boston.

WILLIAM A. HEINEMAN is vice president of academic and student affairs at Northern Essex Community College in Massachusetts.

2

Understanding one's competitive stance in a globally competitive environment provides the requisite awareness to maintain both competitive edge and institutional responsiveness. In this chapter, three case studies are presented to provide examples of ways in which strategic scanning can enhance the academic program development process and how offices of institutional research may assist in launching potentially distinctive academic degrees.

Developing Distinctive Degrees

Lester F. Goodchild, Crystal Renée Chambers, Sydney Freeman, Jr.

The rise of neoinstitutionalism (Powell & DiMaggio, 1991) has captured the imaginations of academics, administrators, and organizational theorists during the past several decades. The Powell and DiMaggio book and similar efforts have described new sociological ways to understand the development of institutions and their contributions to society. Yet the role of such efforts in organizational change through strategic planning to promote program quality (Fairweather & Brown, 1991) and distinctiveness has not been developed fully. Recent commentators (Hendrickson, Lane, Harris, & Dorman, 2013; Toma, 2011) point to using competitive strategy as a way of furthering institutional distinctiveness, mission, and values. Linking strategic planning and competitive strategy to local and regional degree scanning provides campus planners and leaders with a new way to initiate and sustain unique degree program development. This chapter offers a theoretical exploration of key terms, how institutional strategy and strategic planning interrelate, and how strategic degree scanning can be conducted by institutional research offices. With such scanning, institutions have a better chance to create and sustain institutional degree and programmatic distinctiveness. Aggregate cases from Iowa State University, University of Denver, and Santa Clara University are presented to provide examples of the ways in which strategic scanning can enhance the academic program development process.

The Quest for Distinctiveness—A Theoretical Exploration

Many higher education commentators and researchers have sought to explore how to create institutional distinctiveness. These studies began

New Directions for Institutional Research, no. 168 © 2016 Wiley Periodicals, Inc.
Published online in Wiley Online Library (wileyonlinelibrary.com) • DOI: 10.1002/ir.20159

when University of California at Los Angeles Professor Burton Clark published *The Distinctive College* in 1970. His higher education historical and sociological work on how Antioch, Reed, and Swarthmore colleges became distinctive colleges during the late 19th and 20th centuries showed how presidents and faculty created institutional sagas over several decades through the dedicated belief that their faculty roles and approaches to teaching attracted new students. In each case, this required a "radical transformation" in the way the colleges had operated due to a crisis (Clark, 1970/1992, p. vii). In other words, these three demonstrated a unique way of performing their activities that led to them becoming perceived as distinctive institutions. Appropriately for this chapter, this involved new ways of teaching their academic degree programs.

One of the first attempts to apply this concept to other types of colleges came when Barbara K. Townsend edited *A Search for Institutional Distinctiveness* (Townsend, 1989a), an issue of *New Directions for Community Colleges*. In that issue, she and her colleagues reviewed the unique degree and student support programs of community colleges, their use of various inquiry processes for determining distinctive aspects of the institution, efforts to collect various types of data, integration of these into the strategic planning process, demonstration of the institutional benefits from undertaking this approach using short and long case studies, and finally their assessment of the various strengths and weaknesses of this approach.

In her own chapter, Townsend (1989b) sought to explore how institutions can create distinctiveness through their academic programs. She chose two major ways this can happen: empirical and perceptual. An empirical distinctiveness occurs when the institution offers unique academic programs that other institutions in the area or region do not have. On the other hand, a perceptual distinctiveness may happen when students believe that faculty and staff at a particular institution show concern for students' academic progress and well-being—more so than faculty and staff do at other institutions. Overall, Townsend believed that greater distinctiveness will occur when academic leaders are able to align their empirical and perceptual distinctiveness toward a stronger institutional focus on their degree or student support programs, or what might be considered more broadly strengthening their missions. This analytical approach reflected the institutional changes that Clark (1970/1992) found embodied in his three colleges. Critical to Townsend's ideas was how comparisons between and among institutions can reveal unique characteristics. This critical factor represents a significant step in a process that can lead to creating distinctiveness in the institution's mission. By attending to distinctiveness campus leaders might strengthen one aspect of an institution in a planning process that would differentiate it from others and seek through program development greater distinctiveness. Townsend put it more explicitly:

> Developing empirically distinctive programs involves obvious, straightforward steps. Identify a community need, plan a program to meet this need, find funding for the program, and market it. Finding the funding is probably the major task and may be a Herculean one nowadays in some communities and states. However, if institutional leaders can find the money to establish empirically distinctive programs, whether they be academic ones or support resources, institutional distinctiveness of a certain type is within their grasp. (p. 30)
>
> In other words, planning is critical to bringing together and aligning the empirical and perceptual aspects of the institution's goals. She believed that campus leaders through "careful long-range planning" and appropriate "funding" could create institutional distinctiveness (p. 31).

Another chapter in the Townsend issue, "Getting the Facts, Analyzing the Data, Building the Case for Institutional Distinctiveness" (Ratcliff, 1989) takes this planning effort further. He suggests three major ways to assist the institution in becoming distinctive through more formal approaches. The first approach is to gather data about the institution through analyzing institutional histories and strategic planning studies for institutional facts. Second, by assessing institutional need campus leaders seek to understand the local market need for various educational and degree programs or student support programs. Ratcliff commented about this process in the following way:

> Needs assessments are periodically conducted by a college to determine the demand for various programs and services. Most frequently, needs assessments are used in planning continuing education, establishing the need for new career programs, or documenting service to specific community clientele. A needs assessment can provide an ideal opportunity to analyze and describe institutional distinctiveness as well. (p. 51)

Not surprisingly, he suggested using student surveys as one approach to ascertain what type of programs were needed to enable the institution to become more distinctive to its clientele. Ratcliff then takes this approach one step further. He suggests how "impact studies" can be another way in which the institution can serve the local community by placing "the community college in relation to the larger social, economic, and political communities it serves" (p. 53). These internal and external assessment approaches to determine the reasons for creating institutional distinctiveness offer critical components to developing a sustained approach in which institutions not only differentiate themselves, but also create unique and distinctive programming. Finally, most helpful in Ratcliff's discussion was his call for a third approach in this process by using strategic planning studies that involve assessing the larger institutional environment to see opportunities or threats to program development. In this discussion, he notes critically how environmental scanning provides a necessary component to creating institutional distinctiveness.

> Central to the information-gathering portion of strategic planning is a process called environmental scanning. Through this process, the planning group decides on sources of pertinent information regarding external trends in a variety of areas potentially impacting the college, political, demographic, economic, social, technological, and competitive trends and forces. This information is then used to determine possible threats to the college operation and potential opportunities on which the college may wish to capitalize. Through the extrapolation of future trends, issues, and forces, the college's distinct and unique relationship to its environment is identified, and college goals and direction are given. (pp. 54–55)

Environmental scanning provides a larger picture of the major forces affecting the institution. A key feature of this approach is finding opportunities for development, that is, to create various programs that enhance institutional distinctiveness. What needs are occurring in society that the institution uniquely can meet through its educational and training programs? This late 1980s book offers an interesting look at the then state-of-the-art effort to use developing business planning trends and developments in higher education. This effort would gain more higher education followers and expand during the next decade.

Seeking Greater Use of Management Trends

In 2001, Robert Birnbaum offered the higher education community a new critique of its use of business for-profit approaches for institutional development in the nonprofit world of higher education. Here colleges and universities were seeking to employ business planning and strategies, as best as they were able, to improve their educational offerings and institutional missions. Its telling full title, *Management Fads in Higher Education: Where They Come From, What They Do, Why They Fail* (Birnbaum, 2001), seemed to expose limitations of management approaches for ready application to this different educational sector. Nevertheless, during the 1990s, business approaches had great attraction throughout academe, as institutions struggled with increasingly difficult political and financial realities in their states and regions. The use and benefit of business approaches seemed to provide newer and more sophisticated approaches in striving to create institutional distinctiveness.

One of the acclaimed books among campus leaders during this decade that captured this new business approach was *Strategic Change in Colleges and Universities* (Rowley, Lujan, & Dolence, 1997). Interestingly, here the former president of the University of Northern Colorado teamed up with a business professor from the institution and a strategic planning consultant to use a strategic planning process at this state institution. Their focus was to promote successful institutional change for the benefit of its students, faculty, and, the state. The book detailed the use of strategic planning to improve higher education in the face of its critics and consumers. They opted for a more participative planning approach where various campus groups would be involved in seeking to advance the institution, in becoming more strategic in their actions, and ultimately in linking planning and decision making to key performance indicators, such as undergraduate full-time enrollment, student–faculty ratio, graduation rate, and so on. The authors worked with George Keller, whose *Academic Strategy: The Management Revolution in American Higher Education* (Keller, 1983) had become a major call for institutional change through strategic planning across campuses. Keller was invited to write the "Forward" for *Strategic Change in Colleges and Universities*, and described the rationale for using these more powerful approaches to strategic planning, especially using a strengths, weaknesses, opportunities, and threats (SWOT) adaptive process model (see Bess & Dee, 2008) to advance institutional improvement. Keller praised the Rowley et al. effort because it showed the complete planning process with the integral SWOT approach and how it worked at one institution.

Rowley et al. (1997) put forward a 10-step process to implement the strategic planning effort. Their use of the then-growing popular business SWOT analysis for institutional and environmental scanning allowed them to canvas the institution's strengths, weaknesses, opportunities, and threats as well as to use this technique for analyzing suggested individual ideas that had come from various group brainstorming activities. These internal and external SWOT analyses generated lists of institutional strengths (e.g., prestigious faculty or increasing student applications) and weaknesses (e.g., state funding dependence or poor physical plant) to be considered that were supported by factual information and research. Of course, here is a role played by offices of institutional research.

The SWOT analysis planning approach has remained popular, as Hendrickson et al. (2013) recently contended in their book on academic leadership. They cited one of the most recent reviews of the status of strategic planning in higher education to support this claim. Trainer (2004) lists among the top 10 approaches for higher education strategic planning the use of SWOT analyses. This adaptive planning approach provides the opportunity for campus-wide participative involvement—a goal further shown to assist strategic planning success (Sanaghan, 2009)—as well as internal and external reviews of the environment to encourage, as this chapter contends, greater potential for creating distinctive degree programs on campus.

Together, these studies provide considerable insight into the process of assisting institutions to create distinctive academic degrees and support programs. Essential to this development is a planning process that uses internal and external data (Townsend, 1989a) to perceive the institution's strengths and opportunities to offer academic degrees and programs (Hendrickson et al., 2013; Keller, 1983; Rowley et al., 1997). In this effort, internal and external data through institutional assessment and environmental scanning aid campus leaders in understanding the local, state, and regional competitive institutional realities before developing a strategy for new programs. With comparisons, campus administrators and faculty can develop and launch unique degree and support programs (Goodchild, 2000). Linking these approaches together through a planning process may be called competitive degree and program positioning. Seeking to launch a new effort where there is programmatic space in the local, state, or regional context for responding to educational needs with the initiation and continuation of this activity by campus groups over time (Clark, 1970/1992) enhances the possibility of creating institutional distinctiveness.

Aggregate Cases Studies in Public and Private Higher Education

Crafting distinctive degree and support programming can occur when unique opportunities arise on campus. Short aggregate cases where in program highlights are described (Goodchild, 1991) from Iowa State University College of Education's Leadership Institute for the New Century (LINC), University of Denver's Pioneer Leadership Program (PLP) and Higher Education Program, and Santa Clara University School of Education's Higher Education Program provide insights into creating distinctive degrees and continuing education opportunities. In each case, environmental scanning, institutional data collection, and SWOT analysis were utilized in an effort to develop degrees that are distinctive.

Iowa State University. Higher Education Professor James Ratcliff, at Iowa State University in the late 1980s, identified a growing need to educate and provide professional development opportunities to new leaders for the state community colleges. The College of Education's Higher Education Program focused on doctoral education for community college administrators. Iowa's 15 community colleges lacked any women or persons of color in senior leadership positions. In a discussion with then Assistant Professor Lester Goodchild, he suggested Goodchild meet with a vice president from the Des Moines Area Community College and develop a plan for some type of continuing education program. It turned out that neither the University of Iowa nor the University of Northern Iowa offered any such program, which provided the programming positioning key to move forward with the professional education opportunity. Within several months, the three developed a year-long professional development program that also was supported by their Department of Professional Studies Chair, Larry Ebber. The

Leadership Institute for a New Century (LINC) program received support and approval from Iowa's Board of Education. The first program began with an introductory seminar in May 1989 and 20 administrators, all women, were chosen from the state's community colleges to participate. Later, under Professor Ebber's leadership, men were also admitted in 1999, and participants were able to gain academic credit in their doctoral degree work. Although the LINC topics presented monthly during the academic year have evolved over the years, they include: (a) public policy issues and state and local governance; (b) community college leadership, vision, and organizational structure; (c) presidential decision making; (d) community college mission, goals, and ideas; (e) strategic planning; and (f) educational ethics. Some 26 years later, LINC still offers an extraordinary opportunity for the state's future community college leaders to have a distinctive professional learning opportunity and to receive professional education and training at Iowa State University (LINC, 2012).

Four related planning ideas result from this aggregate case, for they show the importance of environmental scanning: (a) the stated need for greater diversity in community college administrators; (b) awareness of a competitive strategy in the form of a unique education opportunity presenting itself (namely, the other two public universities in the state had no community college degree or continuing education program); (c) the appearance of an empirical distinctiveness opportunity to create a program, as no other state university or other institution intended to offer such a program; and (d) the recognition that a SWOT analysis could have revealed the faculty and academic strengths of the Higher Education Program and the opportunity to gain support from the state's Board of Education to launch this initiative. Overall, such program planning provides a glimpse into the local dynamics of creating a distinctive educational support program.

University of Denver. Two cases involving undergraduate and graduate studies provide further insights into how distinctive opportunities can result from planning and program initiation. In the early 1990s, University of Denver's Dean of Student Life William Schafer explored the possibilities of creating an undergraduate leadership program in the College of Education with then Higher Education Associate Professor Lester Goodchild and Counseling Psychology Associate Professor Patrick Sherry. Schafer was aware of an undergraduate leadership program, the President's Leadership Program, that began at the University of Colorado at Boulder in 1972 (President's Leadership Program, 2015) and thought that the University of Denver could create one for its large residential student population. Their discussions led to 2 years of program and curricular planning that involved graduate faculty across the campus, especially in human communications, business, and education. Ultimately, the Pioneer Leadership Program at the University of Denver began in 1995 as seven graduate faculty brought leadership ideas, theories, and cases to a selected group of undergraduates who resided in their own living and learning center. With the approval of the Undergraduate Council, this 4-year 24-credit minor in leadership studies comprised four different annual themes, namely, campus leadership in the student's first year, community and civic leadership in the second, international leadership for those doing a junior year abroad or diverse community leadership for those remaining in the country, and finally in their senior year, a graduate or professional leadership tied to their major. Initially, 19 first- and second-year students began the program. Its success enabled the next academic year PLP-entering group to number 60 students, who maintained a high persistence rate of 93% over their 4 years. The PLP has become a major leadership force on campus with some 260 students spread over the four undergraduate years as of 2015 (Pioneer Leadership Program, 2015). Celebrating its 20-year anniversary in fall 2015, the PLP represents a distinctive undergraduate minor on this campus.

Since 1969, the College of Education offered a doctoral (Ph.D.) program in Higher Education Administration, part of a national movement to launch 70 such programs since 1893 (Goodchild, 2014). This 90 quarter-credit degree program educated and trained college and university administrators for more senior positions at their institutions through courses such as current issues in higher education, leadership and administration, history of higher education, financing higher education, higher education and the law, etc. When then Associate Professor Lester Goodchild assumed the role of coordinator of the program in 1990, he sought to expand the program to add concentrations linked to specific career emphases in higher education. Discussions with his colleagues led to the development of two major four-course sequences in postsecondary public policy and adult studies. With only one other K–12 educational leadership doctoral program with several higher education courses at the University of Colorado Denver, a unique opportunity to expand the public policy concentration presented itself. In large part, this occurred because Denver and Boulder had the largest concentrations of higher education public policy agencies outside of Washington, DC with the Western Interstate Commission for Higher Education, the State Higher Education Executive Officers, the National Center for Higher Education Management Systems, Education Commission of the States, the National Council of State Legislatures, and the Western Governors Association. Moreover, the state legislature was in Denver. Inquiry among some of the senior leaders of these agencies, who had doctorates in higher education and were interested in team teaching, provided the opportunity to create one core course in public policy as well as four concentration courses in national systems of higher education, state systems and boards of higher education, state policy making and the legislature, and higher education policy analysis from the mid-1990s through 2003 (Goodchild, 2014). These courses were approved by the College's Curriculum Committee and endorsed by its faculty. Denver's Higher

Education Program offered more public policy courses than any other degree program in the country, giving it a distinctive, although short-lived, stature.

Related planning ideas in these two academic degree programs at the University of Denver showed how distinctive programmatic opportunities occurred through collaboration with faculty and external colleagues. Lack of any major higher education program in the local or regional area, the internal expertise to offer higher education courses, and the use of environmental scanning to determine the extensive public policy expertise in the region provided useful information to develop program ideas, foster collaboration, and secure authorization from appropriate university governance groups. Key program positioning for both the undergraduate and graduate degrees enabled their initiation, embodiment, and persistence over time (Clark, 1970/1992)—more so with the PLP than with the doctoral degree concentration—thereby creating the possibility for institutional distinctiveness.

Santa Clara University. In the early 2000s, the School of Education, Counseling Psychology, and Pastoral Ministries at the Jesuit Santa Clara University approved the creation of a 45 quarter-unit higher education administration master's degree program. Its initial leadership by Edward Myers, a former Vice President for Student Life at West Valley Community College, provided a unique opportunity to educate and train college support staff in the San Francisco Bay–San Jose area—no other higher education program existed. When its new Dean and Higher Education Professor Lester Goodchild arrived on campus in 2006, there was a unique opportunity to expand the program with more local faculty expertise. Both Myers and Goodchild reviewed the favorable empirical and perceptual educational need for such a program in the region and expanded its core, concentration, and internship courses, such as human resources, law, and finance (Santa Clara University School of Education, n.d.). As its reputation grew, its enrollment almost doubled to 50 master's students. In large part, this administrative program assisted Stanford University professional staff in nearby Palo Alto, who were seeking an applied master's degree with specialized courses that were not available in Stanford's Graduate School of Education. The degree program lasted until 2011, when new Santa Clara University strategic plans downsized its education programs to focus on teacher education and school administration.

Planning considerations in this master's degree expansion related to both the empirical and perceptual educational need for a more applied administrative program in the region. Environmental scanning revealed sufficient need for training local university and college support staff. Increasing faculty expertise enabled the program to offer a broader range of appropriate courses. Growing distinctiveness attracted more student enrollments. This aggregate case points to how analyzing competitive programs, scanning environments, and having sufficient faculty expertise can encourage empirical and perceptual distinctive degree development.

Competitive Degree and Programming Positioning to Achieve Distinctive Status

Each of the cases exemplifies competitive degree and programming positioning in an effort to seek distinctive status, encompassing strategies of environmental scanning, institutional data collection, and SWOT analyses. Environmental scanning was used to determine programmatic need. There was an absence of doctoral programs in Iowa and Denver and a practitioner oriented program at Santa Clara. Doctoral programs at Iowa State and Santa Clara were also built in response to local demands, and the general demand for leadership education resulted in the undergraduate program at Denver. In addition to environment scanning, institutional data collection in each of the cases required an internal assessment of the resources needed to institute and sustain an academic program. A key resource, and usually the most expensive resource over time, is that of faculty. Iowa State built their program upon an energetic assistant professor guided by senior professor through the program development process as well as the expertise of faculty already within the department. Similarly, at Santa Clara, the program was built upon faculty expertise. At Denver, the undergraduate program drew faculty from across academic disciplines to deliver an innovative program of study, and the doctoral program made use of local higher education policy expertise.

Although SWOT analyses are retroactive here, faculty members were an asset, a key programmatic strength in each. Collaboration was important as well. Iowa State had the endorsement of the Higher Education Board and, through the undergraduate program at Denver, the support of student affairs personnel. The graduate program at Denver had access to top policy makers in higher education. In terms of weaknesses, Santa Clara's mission was better aligned with K–12 teacher education and was at a competitive disadvantage when other programs in the area grew. By contrast, the situation at Iowa State was the strongest, as it represented programmatic expansion from an already active higher education administrative program. The undergraduate program at Denver was able to push through competition with the program at Boulder. By contrast, although the PhD program at Denver continues, the specific focus on public policy waned, although public policy continues as an important component.

The important point is for individual programs to take advantage of the local and regional context in order to create programs that are distinctive. Even as guidelines for the development of higher education master's (Bush et al., 2010) and doctoral programs (Council for the Advancement of Higher Education Programs, 2015) are developed, the presence of guidelines does not implicate the homogenization of higher education programs. Instead, distinctiveness here means having an ability to stand out, which is of increasing importance, as programs are no longer compete merely regionally, but also nationally and even globally. Institutional research (IR) offices can and should be employed to assess internal assets, and scan the external environment for both programmatic vacuums and student or industry demand. IR offices can also provide data needed for a rigorous SWOT assessment. Understanding one's competitive stance in a globally competitive environment provides the requisite awareness to maintain both competitive edge and institutional responsiveness. With that awareness, programs can work toward garnering internal and external resources to support sustainability.

References

Bess, J. L., & Dee, J. R. (2008). *Understanding college and university organization: Theories for effective policy and practice*. Sterling, VA: Stylus Publications.

Birnbaum, R. (2001). *Management fads in higher education: Where they come from, what they do, why they fail*. San Francisco, CA: Jossey Bass.

Bush, V. B. et al. (2010). *A commitment to quality: Guidelines for higher education administration and leadership preparation programs at the masters degree level. A proposal from the Executive Committee and the Ad Hoc Committee on Guidelines of the Council for the Advancement of Higher Education Programs*. Retrieved from http://www.ashe.ws/images/CAHEPLeadershipProgramGuidelines.pdf

Clark, B. R. (1970/1992). *The distinctive college*. New Brunswick, NJ: Transaction Publishers. (Original work published 1970)

Council for the Advancement of Higher Education Programs. (2015). *A commitment to scanning quality and professional practice: Voluntary guidelines for higher education administration preparation programs at the doctoral degree level-working draft (ed.)*. Las Vegas, NV: S. Freeman, Jr. & L. F. Goodchild.

Fairweather, J. S., & Brown, D. F. (1991). Dimensions of academic program quality. *The Review of Higher Education*, *14*(2), 155–176.

Goodchild, L. F. (1991). *Public policy dangers facing public universities: A century of research*. Paper presented at the American Educational Research Association, Chicago, IL.

Goodchild, L. F. (2000). *Creating institutional distinctiveness in private higher education: Linking mission, leadership, planning, and decision making*. Invited symposium paper presented at the 10th Annual Oxford University Roundtable on Leadership and Educational Policy. Oxford, UK.

Goodchild, L. F. (2014). Higher education as a field of study: Its history, degree programs, associations, and national guidelines. In S. Freeman, Jr., L. S. Hagedorn, L. F. Goodchild, and D. A. Wright (eds.), *Advancing Higher Education as a Field of Study: In Quest of Doctoral Guidelines—Commemorating 120 Years of Excellence* (pp. 13–50). Sterling, VA: Stylus Publications.

Hendrickson, R. M., Lane, J. E., Harris, J. T., & Dorman, R. H. (2013). *Academic leadership and governance of higher education: A guide for trustees, leaders, and aspiring leaders of two- and four-year institutions*. Sterling, VA: Stylus Publications.

Keller, G. (1983). *Academic strategy: The management revolution in American higher education*. Baltimore, MD: Johns Hopkins University Press.

Leadership Institute for a New Century (LINC). (2012). Community College Leadership Program, Leadership Institute for a New Century (LINC). Retrieved from http://www.cclp.hs.iastate.edu/academics/linc.php

Powell, W. W., & DiMaggio, P. J. (Eds.). (1991). *The new institutionalism in organizational analysis*. Chicago, IL: University of Chicago Press.
Pioneer Leadership Program. (2015). *Lead*. Retrieved from http://www.du.edu/leadership/lead/index.html
President's Leadership Program. (2015). *About*. Retrieved from http://www.presidentsleadershipclass.org/about/history_overview
Ratcliff, J. (1989). Getting the facts, analyzing the data, building the case for institutional distinctiveness. *New Directions for Community Colleges*, *65*, 45–58.
Rowley, D. J., Lujan, H. D., & Dolence, M. G. (1997). *Strategic change in colleges and universities: Planning to survive and prosper*. San Francisco, CA: Jossey Bass.
Sanaghan, P. (2009). *Collaborative strategic planning in higher education*. Washington, DC: National Association of College and University Business Officers.
Santa Clara University School of Education 2008–2009. (n.d.). Available from Santa Clara University, 500 El Camino Real, Santa Clara, CA 95053.
Toma, J. D. (2011). *Managing the entrepreneurial university: Legal issues and commercial realities*. New York, NY: Routledge.
Townsend, B. K. (1989a). A search for institutional distinctiveness: Overviews of process and possibilities. *New Directions for Community Colleges*, *65*, 23–32.
Townsend, B. K. (Ed.). (1989b). A search for institutional distinctiveness. *New Directions for Community Colleges*, *65*.
Trainer, J. F. (2004). Models and tools for strategic planning. *New Directions for Institutional Research*, *123*, 129–138.

LESTER F. GOODCHILD was the distinguished professor of International and Comparative Education at University of Massachusetts at Boston.

CRYSTAL RENÉE CHAMBERS is an associate professor of Educational Leadership, Higher Education Concentration at East Carolina University.

SYDNEY FREEMAN, JR. is an associate professor of Higher Education Leadership at the University of Idaho.

3

Community colleges have been challenged to increase their graduation, transfer, and general success rates. Because they serve the largest proportion of nontraditional students and students of color, their participation in programs to enhance the number of college graduates contributes to social equity and justice. One of the biggest obstacles has been students who enter the developmental pipeline and never emerge to the college level, and hence cannot qualify to graduate or transfer. This chapter speaks to several governmental and nongovernmental initiatives to assist developmental education students achieve academic success.

Developmental, Remedial, and Basic Skills: Diverse Programs and Approaches at Community Colleges

Linda Serra Hagedorn, Inna Kuznetsova

The vast array of offerings available at community colleges include courses designed to assist students who desire postsecondary credentials but arrive academically unprepared for college-level mathematics, English, writing, and/or reading. These courses are generally termed *developmental*, but may also be called *remedial* or *below college level*. This chapter speaks to several governmental and nongovernmental initiatives to assist developmental education students achieve academic success. Assessment of the efficacy of these initiatives is within the purview of institutional research offices. A glossary of related terms is available in the Appendix.

Background

Community colleges are often criticized for attempting to be all things to all people. Indeed, community colleges offer a broad set of educational choices that serve a diverse set of students. In fact, nontraditional students far outnumber the traditional college students (American Association of Community Colleges [AACC], 2015b). The term *nontraditional* includes students who are employed, supporting their families, have a disability, and/or are veterans, in addition to students who are older or are people of color. Most community colleges offer a wide array of liberal arts courses designed for transfer to the 4-year sector as well as an assortment of vocational and certificate programs and may confer a long list of degree types.

In addition to the credit programs, most community colleges also offer noncredit education. In fact, for some colleges, noncredit enrollment may exceed the for-credit (Van Noy, Jacobs, Korey, Bailey, & Hughes, 2008). Some noncredit courses students take are for personal enrichment, but on the noncredit side are also programs that offer continuing education units, and in some cases programs such as the GED (Ryder & Hagedorn, 2012), basic literacy and numeracy skills for adults, and English as a Second Language coursework. According to the American Association of Community Colleges (AACC, 2015a), about 40% of the community college head count, or more than five million students, are enrolled as noncredit.

Developmental Education

Given the community college mission of providing "inclusive institutions that welcome all who desire to learn, regardless of wealth, heritage, or previous academic experience" (AACC, 2015c, paragraph 1) developmental education has already become huge and costly, and is growing. The annual cost of developmental education at community colleges is estimated at about four billion dollars (Scott-Clayton & Rodriguez, 2012). Despite the high costs, McCabe (2003) identified developmental education as a societal benefit. Two-thirds or more of all community college students enter their institutions with weak academic skills that may prevent them from postsecondary success (Bailey, 2009). Although all students who might benefit from developmental coursework will not enroll in the courses, according to the latest National Postsecondary Student Aid Study (NPSAS) data, about 40% of all community college students in 2011–12 were enrolled in at least one developmental course (U.S. Department of Education, 2011). This includes students identified as English as a Second Language (ESL), who in institutions without academic ESL coursework are directed to general adult basic education or regular developmental English courses, typically without academic credit (Hagedorn & Li, in press). The placement of ESL students within developmental studies is problematic, given differences in students' needs (Hodara, Jaggars, & Karp, 2012). Also overidentified are students who take placement tests like the ACT or SAT, but do not approach the tests with an understanding of their importance or high-stakes nature, and fail to prepare or study as university-hopeful students (Shelton & Brown, 2008). True to their missions, community colleges are the postsecondary sector most engaged with developmental education. State and/or institutional policies of many 4-year universities and colleges prohibit admission of students requiring remediation and often direct such students to community colleges (Jacobs, 2012).

The developmental education costs to students accrue in time, money, and energy (Hagedorn, Lester, & Cypers, 2010). Low completion rates

Table 3.1. Example of Hierarchical Levels in Developmental and College-Level Education

Level	*Definition*
0—Remedial	Lowest level. In some districts or states is part of the adult basic education offering. Examples include pre-algebra, math fundamentals, and arithmetic.
1—Basic	Low high school level. Examples include basic elementary algebra and introduction to algebra.
2—Intermediate	Continuation of high school level. Examples include intermediate algebra and essentials of geometry.
3—Advanced/transfer	College level. Examples: college algebra, trigonometry, and calculus.

among developmental students are well documented (Hagedorn & Lester, 2006; Melguizo, Hagedorn, & Cypers, 2008; Radford, Berkner, Wheeless, & Shepherd, 2010). Reasons for low completion rates are many, but include the concept of developmental climb (Hagedorn & DuBray, 2010; Hagedorn & Lester, 2006). Table 3.1 uses course titles taken from mathematics as examples, but hierarchical levels apply to other developmental subjects. Although the number of levels in each college varies and is a topic of concern, study, and refinement, most colleges employ a levels structure to define student placement. Once a student climbs through the levels, she or he is college ready for academic, for- credit courses and academic programs. Students who do not complete academic programming (a) must still repay student loan debt, and (b) may represent an inefficient use of Pell or other grant aid (Fernandez, Barone, & Klepfer, 2014). In response to the high costs of developmental education, both governmental and nongovernmental actors are engaging in policy and other interventions to turn the developmental education tide.

Enrollment/Admissions Initiatives

Texas. With their Texas Success Initiative (TSI), Texas mandates that all students enrolling in public postsecondary institutions be assessed for readiness in reading, mathematics, and writing unless they qualify for an exemption (Texas Higher Education Coordinating Board, 2012). As of fall 2013, the state has standardized one statewide assessment instrument and specific cut-scores that separate student scores into three levels: adult basic education, developmental education, and college ready. The cut-scores, however, will gradually increase through the fall of 2019. The lowest level, adult basic education, is for students with abilities described as "pre-high school level" (Texas Higher Education Coordinating Board, n.d.). Critics of this initiative point out that those students classified within adult basic education may not be eligible for the same types of financial aid as those within the developmental structure.

Florida. A senior research associate at Florida State University's Center for Postsecondary Success related that about 78% of all Florida community college students tested during the 2005–06 academic year scored below college level (Ross, 2014). Nevertheless, rather than provide more courses or pursue new ways to remediate community college students, Florida is challenging the need for remediation. The Florida legislation (Education, 2013) follows a 2011 law mandating all 11th graders take a placement test to determine the appropriate coursework in the 12th grade. Students with low test scores are required to take remedial courses during their last year in high school. As of fall 2014, the state of Florida allows students to enroll for college-level courses directly despite placement test score results, placing the onus on students to decide the need for and benefit from developmental education.

California. California Community Colleges enroll more students than any other state and also have the country's largest number of students needing developmental education. Between 70 and 80% of students in the California system test in the developmental level (Basic Skills Initiative, 2007). Despite the attention and funds for developmental education (Basic Skills Initiative, 2009), a 2014 report from the Research and Planning Group for California Community Colleges reports that only 19% of students from the lowest levels of developmental English and 7% of similarly placed students in developmental math enroll in a college-level course within 3 years (Hayward & Willett, 2014).

Tennessee. Supported by the Fund for the Improvement of Postsecondary Education (FIPSE), the state of Tennessee offered the Developmental Studies Redesign Initiative (2006–2009) to promote active-learning strategies and technology-infused curricula to improve developmental math and English (National Center for Academic Transformation, 2006). This was quickly followed by the Complete College Tennessee Act of 2010 (CCTA), designed to work in conjunction with the state's Drive-to-55 plan, which aims to have at least 55% of all Tennessee citizens holding college degree or credential (Tennessee Board of Regents, 2015).

The Tennessee plan consists of two major initiatives: (a) a special math course taken in high school for students testing below college level, and (b) promotion of corequisite enrollment of developmental and college-level courses during the community college first year. Both aspects of the Tennessee plan show evidence of success. A report from the Tennessee Board of Regents (2015) indicates that the early remediation potentially saved more than $6.6 million and the corequisite plan increased the completion of gateway math courses by a factor of 4.

Washington. The State of Washington provides a different example through their Integrated Basic Education and Skills Training (I-BEST) program. I-BEST uniquely addresses workforce training and literacy by combining workplace skills with literacy, promoting the completion of degrees and certificates for students who would otherwise be required to enroll in developmental education (State Board for Community and Technical Colleges [SBCTC], 2015a).

Performance-Based Funding

Developmental education is included in performance-based funding (PBF) formulas in several states including Arkansas, Missouri, North Carolina, Ohio, Texas, Utah, and Washington. There are subtle differences in how the states reward community colleges for developmental education gains. In both Missouri and Utah, a segment of the PBF for community colleges is calculated based on the percentage of students who successfully complete *both* developmental and the first college-level courses in English or math (Legislative Fiscal Analyst, 2014; Missouri Coordinating Board for Higher Education, 2012). In North Carolina, PBF is allocated in part on the developmental student success rate in math and/or English and basic skills student progress (North Carolina Community Colleges, 2014). In Ohio, PBF is accrued when students complete their first developmental course in English and/or math and again when they attempt a college-level course in English and/or math (Ohio Higher Ed, 2015). In Washington, performance-based funding accrues when students complete the sequence (they do not have to enroll in the college-level course) (SBCTC, 2015b). Regardless of the funding formula, the inclusion of developmental education success is designed to reward colleges for finding the appropriate structures to support student success.

Prematriculation Programs

Because success rates for developmental courses are generally low, some colleges, states, and high schools have initiated a variety of interventions to assist students attain academic performance at college level while they are still enrolled in high school or during the summer following graduation. Realizing a misalignment between high school and college expectations, some states, like Florida, and select districts require student assessments in the 11th grade to identify students who would test into developmental levels and then provide supports and instruction during the 12th grade (Bangser, 2008).

Bridge Programs. Bridge programs are a common prematriculation intervention, generally experiences scheduled between high school and college with the goal of creating a structure that prepares students for the academic and social rigors of college (Edgecombe, Cormier, Bickerstaff, & Barragan, 2013; Sherer & Grunow, 2010). These programs are generally 5–10 weeks in duration but may be as long as the full summer (Sherer & Grunow, 2010).

Boot Camp. A boot camp can be viewed as a shorter, more intense bridge program. Although there are specialty boot camps to train students in specific career or vocational skills, the major focus of most community college boot camps is for students to score higher on placement exams, allowing them to place in a higher developmental level or completely bypass developmental courses. Other goals may include developing positive study skills, and gaining overall "college knowledge." Many boot camps are free for participants but supported by grants or other temporary funds, which makes them difficult to maintain. The evidence of effectiveness of boot camps is mixed (Hodara, 2013), the major criticism being their expense and small service reach.

Curricular Approaches to Developmental Education

Learning Communities. Learning communities promote the development of social and academic support networks as students enroll as a cohort in two or more thematically linked courses as well as participate in other academic and/or social offerings. A common practice is to link a developmental course with a special student success course, or link developmental English with a content course such as history or psychology. Another model, described later in this chapter, is to link a developmental with the college-level course (in English or math) as a way to accelerate students through the developmental pipeline. Some learning communities include tutoring services, supplemental instruction, or other types of related structured study.

Research suggests learning communities promote engagement and strong relationships among the students as well as promote positive student–faculty interactions (Inkelas, Szele'nyi, Soldner, & Brower, 2007; Kuh, 2008). However, the literature on learning communities specifically for developmental students is sparse (Visher, Schneider, Wathington, & Collado, 2010). MDRC conducted a study of five community colleges with learning communities that incorporated developmental English and/or math. The study of about 7,000 developmental students across 174 learning communities found "no impact on persistence, a half-credit impact on credits earned in the targeted subject (English or mathematics), no impact on credits outside that subject, and a half-credit effect on total credits earned" (MDRC, 2012, paragraph 5). The conclusion is that learning communities may produce a modest impact on developmental students.

Learning communities present multiple challenges, and hence have lost some popularity in recent times. First, there is a higher level of management and support required for faculty to work together effectively in preparing joint curriculum—a practice that results in additional workload (that is sometimes paid and sometimes not). Learning communities also present scheduling difficulties for students, who often juggle multiple responsibilities. This challenge too often results in course enrollment numbers being lower than in unlinked sections of the same courses. Additional services, if provided, such as tutoring, add to bottom-line costs.

Student Success Courses. Student success courses are designed to provide community college students with helpful tools and knowledge that will encourage both academic and nonacademic success. The curriculum varies, but generally includes topics such as note-taking, study skills, time management, introduction to the services available on campus, applying for financial aid, and other basic instruction that could be termed "college knowledge." Some colleges view the success course as an elongated orientation. A common practice already mentioned is to link the student success course with one or more developmental courses, creating a learning community. Some colleges make student success courses mandatory for first-semester first-time-in-college students and others mandate it for only students in the developmental sequence. Other colleges offer the course as optional but highly recommended. Success courses are extremely popular and are offered in many 2- and 4-year colleges and universities, with 87% of postsecondary institutions offering a success course or first-year seminar in 2009 (Padgett & Keup, 2011).

Empirical studies provide evidence that these courses are beneficial for students in developmental levels in outcomes such as retention (Schnell & Doetkott, 2003); academic performance (Boudreau & Kromrey, 1994), college navigational skills (O'Gara, Karp, & Hughes, 2009), and transfer (Zeidenberg, Jenkins, & Calcagno, 2007) . However, there is also evidence that the impacts may be short-term (Karp et al., 2012; Rutschow, Cullinan, & Welbeck, 2012; Weiss, Brock, Sommo, Rudd, & Turner, 2011).

Modularization. Some colleges have turned to new ways to present the developmental content. Rather than present the curriculum packaged in the traditional semester or quarter format, content is presented in standalone modules, allowing students to participate only in those modules with materials they still need to learn as determined by placement tests. By eliminating content already understood, students accelerate by decreasing their time through the developmental pipeline. Often the modularized approach is administered in a math lab that is based on mastery and allows students to work at their own pace.

Since 2012, developmental math has been presented in modularized format in all 23 of Virginia's community colleges (VCC). Students must take the Virginia Placement Test to identify which of the nine modules contain content still left to learn. Each module is presented as a one-credit 4-week course. According to the VCC Progress Report (Virginia Community Colleges, 2015), the redesign of mathematics has contributed to several success goals, including an increased number of students completing the developmental math sequence in 1 year.

Curricular Substitutions. Another approach to encouraging student success through developmental education is to offer an alternative to the traditional courses. Beginning in 2010, the Carnegie Foundation for the Advancement of Teaching initiated the Community College Pathways program that promotes two alternatives to developmental math (Carnegie Foundation, 2015). Alternative one, called Quantway, is curriculum preparing students for college-level math through a focus on quantitative reasoning. Alternative two, called Statway, is curriculum preparing students for occupational degrees by including instruction on causal reasoning and statistics. According to evaluations published by the Carnegie Foundation (Van Campen, Sowers, & Strother, 2013), both courses produced positive outcomes, including completion rates of over 50%.

Online. Despite the research indicating lower student completion rates within online courses compared to their traditional face-to-face counterparts (Lee & Choi, 2011), some community colleges offer developmental courses in an online format. Although study of specifically developmental online courses is sparse, a study among the Virginia Colleges recorded huge negative differences in the completion rates for students taking their developmental coursework online; a decrement of 24 percentage points for English and 19 percentage points for math (Jaggars & Xu, 2010).

Acceleration. Believing that a major reason so few students complete the developmental sequence is the extended time it takes students to climb through the developmental levels, some college policymakers advocate fast tracks. Modularizing, as discussed earlier, can accelerate the developmental process, but there are other formats of acceleration such as compression, mainstreaming, and course amalgamations.

Some colleges compress developmental content from a 16-week semester into an 8-week or shorter time frame. Of course, as calendar time decreases, the time in class increases, as compression does not necessarily mean that content has been eliminated. In theory, compression allows students to complete more developmental levels in a single semester, hence accelerating the process. Although compression is the main difference between these minicourses and their full-semester counterparts, typically the compressed version also includes more technology or enhanced pedagogy to maintain student interest during longer class times.

In an attempt to shorten the developmental pipeline, some colleges combine key content from developmental levels into fewer levels. This process of amalgamation or blending of, for example, three levels into two, requires the elimination of some content, less time on some concepts, higher speed in coverage, or a combination of methods.

Another and perhaps the most controversial of all accelerations is mainstreaming. Mainstreaming allows students in the highest level of remediation to co-enroll with the college-level course. For example, a student in the highest level of remediation in English would co-enroll in English 101. Developmental mainstreaming was first practiced by the Community College of Baltimore County in 2007 in a program called the Accelerated

Learning Program (ALP). Students in ALP co-enroll in both developmental and college-level English courses that are taught by the same instructor. Evaluations of the program indicate that ALP students were more likely to complete both English 101 and 102 than developmental students who did not participate in the program (Cho, Kopko, Jenkins, & Jaggars, 2012).

Overall, the evidence of effectiveness of accelerated programs is mixed (Edgecombe, 2011). Some studies find positive outcomes, whereas others identify methodological weaknesses (Daniel, 2000).

Special Nongovernmental Initiatives. Developmental education in community colleges has fomented a great deal of discussion and debate among many audiences. There is no shortage of articles, research, or editorials about the costs, the low success rates, and the broad search for solutions. Many funding sources and philanthropic organizations provide grants for programs designed to alleviate or decrease the number of students or the time it takes to climb up the developmental pipeline. The Bill & Melinda Gates Foundation alone has invested over a half billion dollars toward student success in community colleges with the goal of increasing the number of students who complete a degree or credential (Sturgis, 2014). Major programs and whole nonprofit organizations are institutionalized around these needs. We provide some information about a few of the major programs or initiatives.

Achieving the Dream (ATD). Begun in 2004, ATD has become the largest initiative in the country focusing on closing the achievement gaps that separate students of color and low-income students from those with a greater likelihood to succeed (Achieving the Dream, 2015). After more than a decade, ATD can boast of supporting success initiatives at close to 200 community college campuses across 34 states. The initiative has recently evolved into a nonprofit organization led by a board of directors. Although the developmental climb is not the only goal of ATD colleges, they recognize that student success depends on the college's ability to provide the necessary support and guidance for students who require developmental instruction. The evaluation of outcomes for this large national initiative are mixed. Although there are success stories of colleges increasing the number of students who climb up developmental levels, large-scale evaluations of graduations and transfers overall remain flat (Jenkins, Ellwein, Wachen, Kerrigan, & Cho, 2009; Mayer et al., 2014). It may be that ATD initiatives have not touched a sufficient number of students to move the needle for the colleges as a whole.

Getting Past Go. Getting Past Go is a national initiative created through a collaboration with The Education Commission of the States. The initiative seeks not only to support research on effective developmental education practices but also to support states to adopt the policies and practices that result in goal attainment (Getting Past Go, n.d.).

Completion by Design (CPD). CPD, funded by the Bill & Melinda Gates Foundation, is an initiative focused on increasing the completion and graduation rates of low-income community college students. Currently working in Florida, North Carolina, and Ohio, CPD advocates the implementation of strategies designed to assist students to climb through the developmental levels and program completion (Completion by Design, 2015).

Complete College America (CCA). CCA has formed an alliance of states to enhance college completion. Included among its five "game changers" is the promotion of corequisite remediation (or mainstreaming). The organization also promotes performance-based funding, structured schedules, and guided pathways to success (Complete College America, 2014).

Conclusions

Community colleges are challenged to increase their graduation, transfer, and general success rates. Because they serve the largest proportion of nontraditional and students of color, their participation in programs to enhance the number of college graduates contributes to social equity and justice. One of the biggest obstacles has been students who enter the developmental pipeline and never emerge to the college level, and hence cannot qualify to graduate or transfer. If the United States is to achieve the goal of 10 million more college graduates and opportunities for every American to complete 1 year or more of higher education or advanced training in his/her lifetime by 2020, it is clear that finding better answers to how to remediate community college students is key, and institutional research offices can be helpful in both framing challenges and identifying solutions. Despite the many programs and initiatives, it is safe to say that we have not found the "silver bullet."

We are left with many questions. What is the future of developmental education? Who should take the responsibility and shoulder the burden? Should the onus be on the high schools to assess and provide evidence of college readiness prior to providing high school degrees? Should the states or federal governments offer financial incentives or fines for high schools and colleges for their college readiness status? Should strict limits be set for financial aid provided to students while in the developmental pipeline? One certainty in the brave new future world is that the problem will not disappear and will remain an obstacle to increasing the number of college graduates. The good news is that community colleges, for the most part, are not giving up, and as assessment offices within this sector grow in depth and breadth, so too do the possibilities of improving student success. The evidence of so many initiatives and projects indicate the resilience of community colleges and their desire to assist students to success. Again, these institutions have been asked to be all things to all people ... but if community colleges don't do it, who will?

References

Achieving the Dream. (2015). *Helping more community college students achieve.* Retrieved from http://www.achievingthedream.org/.

American Association of Community Colleges (AACC). (2015a). *2015 community college fast facts.* Retrieved from http://www.aacc.nche.edu/AboutCC/Pages/fastfactsfactsheet.aspx

American Association of Community Colleges. (AACC). (2015b). *2015 fact sheet.* Retrieved from http://www.aacc.nche.edu/AboutCC/Documents/FactSheet2015.pdf

American Association of Community Colleges (AACC). (2015c). *About community colleges.* Retrieved from http://www.aacc.nche.edu/AboutCC/Pages/default.aspx

Bailey, T. (2009). *Rethinking developmental education in community college* (Columbia University, Teachers College, Community College Research Center [CCRC] Brief). Retrieved from http://files.eric.ed.gov/fulltext/ED504329.pdf

Bangser, M. (2008). *Preparing high school students for successful transitions to postsecondary education and employment* (Report by the National High School Center). Retrieved from http://betterhighschools.org/docs/PreparingHSStudentsforTransition_073108.pdf

Basic Skills Initiative. (2007). *Basic skills as a foundation for student success in California community colleges.* Retrieved from http://www.cccbsi.org/websites/basicskills/images/basicskills_booklet-2.pdf

Basic Skills Initiative. (2009). *About the project.* Retrieved from http://www.cccbsi.org/about

Boudreau, C. A., & Kromrey, J. D. (1994). A longitudinal study of the retention and academic performance of participants in a freshman orientation course. *Journal of College Student Development*, 45(6), 444–449.

Carnegie Foundation. (2015). *Pathways Improvement Communities.* Retrieved from http://www.carnegiefoundation.org/in-action/pathways-improvement-communities/

Cho, S. W., Kopko, E., Jenkins, D., & Jaggars, S. S. (2012). *New evidence of success for community college remedial English students: Tracking the outcomes of students in the Accelerated Learning Program (ALP).* (Columbia University, Teachers College, Community College Research Center [CCRC] Working Paper No. 53). Retrieved from http://ccrc.tc.columbia.edu/media/k2/attachments/ccbc-alp-student-outcomes-follow-up.pdf

Complete College America. (2014). *The game changers.* Retrieved from http://completecollege.org/

Completion by Design. (2015). *Our approach.* Retrieved from http://www.completionbydesign.org/our-approach

Daniel, E. L. (2000). A review of time-shortened courses across disciplines. *College Student Journal, 34*(2), 298–308.

Edgecombe, N. (2011). *Accelerating the academic achievement of students referred to developmental education* (Columbia University, Teachers College, Community College Research Center [CCRC] Working Paper No. 30). Retrieved from http://ccrc.tc.columbia.edu/media/k2/attachments/accelerating-academic-achievement-students.pdf

Edgecombe, N., Cormier, M.S., Bickerstaff, S., & Barragan, M. (2013). *Strengthening developmental education reforms: Evidence on implementation efforts from the Scaling Innovation project* (Columbia University, Teachers College, Community College Research Center [CCRC] Working Paper No. 61). Retrieved from http://ccrc.tc.columbia.edu/media/k2/attachments/strengthening-developmental-education-reforms.pdf

Education, State Bill 1720. (2013). Retrieved from https://www.flsenate.gov/Session/Bill/2013/1720/BillText/Filed/HTML

Fernandez, C., Barone, S., & Klepfer, K. (2014). *Developmental education and student debt: Remediation's uncertain impact on financial and academic outcomes* (TG Research and Analytical Services). Retrieved from https://www.tgslc.org/pdf/Developmental-Education-and-Student-Debt.pdf

Getting Past Go. (n.d.). *Project description*. Retrieved from http://gettingpastgo.org/about/project-description/

Hagedorn, L. S., & DuBray, D. (2010). Math and science success and nonsuccess: Journeys within the community college. *Journal of Women and Minorities in Science and Engineering, 16*(1), 31–50.

Hagedorn, L. S., & Lester, J. (2006). Hispanic community college students and the transfer game: Strikes, misses, and grand experiences. *Community College Journal of Research and Practice, 30*(10), 827–853.

Hagedorn, L. S., Lester, J., & Cypers, S. J. (2010). C problem: Climb or catastrophe. *Community College Journal of Research and Practice, 34*(3), 240–255.

Hagedorn, L. S., & Li, R. (in press). English instruction at community colleges: The language bridge to the U.S. In L. Tran (Ed.), *Internationalization in vocational education and training: Transnational perspectives*. New York, NY: Springer.[Hayward, C., & Willett, T. (2014). *Curricular redesign and gatekeeper completion*. Retrieved from http://rpgroup.org/sites/default/files/CAP_Summary_Final_May2014.pdf

Hodara, M. (2013). *Improving students' college math readiness* (Education Northwest). Retrieved from http://educationnorthwest.org/sites/default/files/resources/improving%20college%20math%20readiness_0.pdf

Hodara, M., Jaggars, S., & Karp. M. (2012). *Improving developmental education assessment and placement: Lessons from community colleges across the country* (Columbia University, Teachers College, Community College Research Center [CCRC] Working Paper No. 51). Retrieved from http://ccrc.tc.columbia.edu/publications/developmental-education-assessment-placement-scan.html

Inkelas, K. K., Szele'nyi, K., Soldner, M., & Brower, A. M. (2007). *National study of living learning programs: 2007 report of findings*. College Park, MD: University of Maryland. Retrieved from http://drum.lib.umd.edu/bitstream/1903/8392/1/2007%20NSLLP%20Final%20Report.pdf

Jacobs, J. (2012, January 13). States push remedial education to community colleges. *U.S. News and World Report*. Retrieved from www.usnews.com/education/best-colleges/articles/2012/01/13/states-push-remedial-education-to-community-colleges

Jaggars, S. S., & Xu, D. (2010). *Online learning in the Virginia community college system*. Retrieved from http://ccrc.tc.columbia.edu/media/k2/attachments/online-learning-virginia.pdf

Jenkins, D., Ellwein, T., Wachen, J., Kerrigan, M. R., & Cho, S. W. (2009). *Achieving the Dream colleges in Pennsylvania and Washington State: Early progress toward building a culture of evidence*. Retrieved from http://ccrc.tc.columbia.edu/publications/atd-pennsylvania-washington-early-progress.html

Karp, M. M., Bickerstaff, S., Rucks-Ahidiana, Z., Bork, R. H., Barragan, M.,& Edgecombe, N. (2012). *College 101 courses for applied learning and student success* (Columbia University, Teachers College, Community College Research Center [CCRC] Working Paper No. 49). Retrieved from http://ccrc.tc.columbia.edu/publications/college-101-applied-learning-student-success.html

Kuh, G. D. (2008). *High-impact educational practices: What are they, who has access to them, and why they matter.* Washington, DC: Association of American Colleges and Universities.

Lee, Y., & Choi, J. (2011). A review of online course dropout research: Implications for practice and future research. *Educational Technology Research & Development, 59*(5), 593–618.

Legislative Fiscal Analyst. (2014). *Budget for the State of Utah and related appropriations*. Retrieved from http://le.utah.gov/interim/2014/pdf/00003542.pdf

McCabe, R. (2003).*Yes we can: A community college guide for developing America's underprepared*. Washington, DC: Community College Press.

Mayer, A. K., Cerna, O., Cullinan, D., Fong, K., Rutschow, E. Z., & Jenkins, D. (2014). Moving ahead with institutional change: Lessons from the first round of Achieving the Dream community colleges. Retrieved from: http://files.eric.ed.gov/fulltext/ED546648.pdf.

MDRC. (2012). *What have we learned about learning communities at community colleges?* Retrieved from http://www.mdrc.org/publication/what-have-we-learned-about-learning-communities-community-colleges

Melguizo, T., Hagedorn, L. S., & Cypers, S. (2008). The need for remedial/developmental education and the cost of community college transfer: Calculations from a sample of California community college transfers. *The Review of Higher Education*, *31*(4), 401–431.

Missouri Coordinating Board for Higher Education. (2012). *Performance funding model.* Retrieved from http://dhe.mo.gov/documents/PerformanceFundingReport.pdf

National Center for Academic Transformation. (2006). *State and system course redesign.* Retrieved from http://www.thencat.org/States/TBR.htm

North Carolina Community Colleges. (2014). *Success NC: Performance measures and funding.* Retrieved from http://www.successnc.org/initiatives/performance-measures-funding

O'Gara, L., Karp, M. M., & Hughes, K. L. (2009). Student success courses in the community college. *Community College Review*, *36*(3), 195–218.

Ohio Higher Ed. (2015). *Student Success Initiative—Success points.* Retrieved from https://www.ohiohighered.org/content/student_success_initiative_success_points

Padgett, R. D., & Keup, J. R. (2011). *2009 national survey of first-year seminars: Ongoing efforts to support students in transition.* Columbia, SC: University of South Carolina, National Resource Center for the First-Year Experience and Students in Transition.

Radford, A. W., Berkner, L., Wheeless, S. C., & Shepherd, B. (2010). *Persistence and attainment of 2003–04 beginning postsecondary students: After 6 years (NCES 2011–151).* Washington, DC: U.S. Department of Education, Institute of Education Sciences, National Center for Education Statistics.

Ryder, A., & Hagedorn, L.S. (2012). GED and other noncredit courses: The other side of the community college. *New Directions for Institutional Research*, *153*, 21–31.

Ross, J. (2014). Why is Florida ending remedial education for college students? *National Journal.* Retrieved from http://www.nationaljournal.com/next-america/education/why-is-florida-ending-remedial-education-for-college-students-20140825

Rutschow, E. Z., Cullinan, D., & Welbeck, R. (2012). *Keeping students on course: An impact study of a student success course at Guilford Technical Community College.* New York, NY: MDRC.

SBCTC Washington State Board for Community and Technical Colleges (2015a). *I-BEST: Integrated basic education and skills training.* Retrieved from http://www.sbctc.ctc.edu/college/e_integratedbasiceducationandskillstraining.aspx

SBCTC Washington State Board for Community and Technical Colleges. (2015b). *Student achievement initiative.* Retrieved from http://www.sbctc.ctc.edu/college/e_studentachievement.aspx.

Schnell, C. A., & Doetkott, C. D. (2003). First year seminars produce long-term impact. *Journal of College Student Retention*, *4*(4), 377–391.

Scott-Clayton, J., & Rodriguez, O. (2012). *Development, discouragement, or diversion? New evidence on the effects of college remediation* (National Bureau of Economic Research Working Paper 18328). Retrieved from http://www.nber.org/papers/w18328.pdf

Shelton, A., & Brown, R. (2008). *Measuring the alignment of high school and community college math assessments.* Retrieved from http://digitallibrary.usc.edu/cdm/ref/collection/p15799coll127/id/91808

Sherer, J. Z., & Grunow, A. (2010). *90-day cycle: Exploration of math intensives as a strategy to move more community colleges students out of developmental math courses*. Retrieved from http://cdn.carnegiefoundation.org/wp-content/uploads/2010/10/90_day_cycle_boot_camps.pdf

Sturgis, I. (2014). Gates Foundation invests half-billion in success of community college students. *Diverse Issues in Higher Education*. Retrieved from http://diverseeducation.com/article/59973/

Tennessee Board of Regents. (2015). *Fact sheet. The Tennessee Community College System's plan to support the state's completion agenda: Remediation redesign, academic alignment, and structured intervention*. Retrieved from https://www.google.com/url?sa=t&rct=j&q=&esrc=s&source=web&cd=5&ved=0CDwQFjAEahUKEwijwOrn2vTGAhUByj4KHejsA8I&url=http%3A%2F%2Fachievingthedream.org%2Fsystem%2Ffiles_force%2Fresources%2FFact%2520Sheet%2520-%2520Tennessee%2520Community%2520College%2520System%2520(2).docx%3Fdownload%3D1&ei=1a2yVeOBDYGU-wHo2Y-QDA&usg=AFQjCNEn-t-fxlfH9MaOve5EpNtwaT3xJw&sig2=ko9jSG-DbD0DkghITO67eQ&bvm=bv.98717601,d.cWw&cad=rja

Texas Higher Education Coordinating Board. (2012). *Overview Texas Success Initiative*. Retrieved from http://www.google.com/url?sa=t&rct=j&q=&esrc=s&source=web&cd=5&cad=rja&uact=8&ved=0CDkQFjAEahUKEwjJ05GSo93GAhWCez4KHRhFBo0&url=http%3A%2F%2Fwww.thecb.state.tx.us%2Fdownload.cfm%3Fdownloadfile%3D231C15C8-F65B-29E9--9A977770FC198C75%26typename%3DdmF...&ei=c2SmVYnOIoL3-QGYipnoCA&usg=AFQjCNEZ42ZStekgNMyuP8fvHakMGwEYzw&sig2=hmgtuvPuNFbpUXXVgHD80Q&bvm=bv.97653015,d.cWw

Texas Higher Education Coordinating Board. (n.d.). *New Texas Success Initiative Assessment*. Retrieved from http://www.google.com/url?sa=t&rct=j&q=&esrc=s&source=web&cd=7&ved=0CEgQFjAGahUKEwjGq9rLpt3GAhXT_YAKHXdyCrU&url=http%3A%2F%2Fwww.thecb.state.tx.us%2Fdownload.cfm%3Fdownloadfile%3DAD1E748E-DDB1--9FC3--4CE52EADAF41B83C%26typename%3DdmFile%26fieldname%3Dfilename&ei=EWimVYbfJNP7gwT35KmoCw&usg=AFQjCNHl_-bqG1_-BYDytb9K5OIpHvAiFA&sig2=EN2unii69R2pnSrShyjafg&bvm=bv.97653015,d.eXY&cad=rja

U.S. Department of Education, National Center for Education Statistics. (2011). *National Postsecondary Student Aid Study, 2011–12* (NPSAS: 12). Retrieved from: https://nces.ed.gov/pubsearch/pubsinfo.asp?pubid=2013165

Van Campen, J., Sowers, N., & Strother, S. (2013). *Community college pathways: 2012–2013 descriptive report* (Report for the Carnegie Foundation for the Advancement of Teaching). Retrieved from http://www.carnegiefoundation.org/wp-content/uploads/2013/08/CCP_Descriptive_Report_Year_2.pdf

Van Noy, M., Jacobs, J., Korey, S., Bailey, T., & Hughes, K. L. (2008). *Noncredit enrollment in workforce education: State policies and community college practices*. Washington, DC: American Association of Community Colleges. Retrieved from http://www.aacc.nche.edu/Publications/Reports/Documents/noncredit.pdf

Virginia Community Colleges. (2015). *Rethink: Reengineering Virginia's community colleges. Reengineering progress report: Redesign developmental education*. Retrieved from http://rethink.vccs.edu/progress/redesign-developmental-education/

Visher, M. G., Schneider, E., Wathington, H., & Collado, H. (2010). *Scaling up learning communities*. Retrieved from http://www.mdrc.org/sites/default/files/scaling_up_learning_communities_fr.pdf

Weiss, M. J., Brock, T., Sommo, C., Rudd, T., & Turner, M. C. (2011). *Serving community college students on probation: Four-year findings from Chaffey College's Opening Doors program*. New York, NY: MDRC.

Zeidenberg, M., Jenkins, D., & Calcagno, J. C. (2007, June). *Do student success courses actually help community college students succeed?* (Columbia University, Teachers College, Community College Research Center [CCRC] Working Paper No. 36). Retrieved from http://academiccommons.columbia.edu/catalog/ac:157602

Appendix: Glossary of Terms

Term	*Definition*
Acceleration	Practices and programs that decrease the time for remediation. Can include modularization, co-requisite enrollment in college-level courses or compressed course designs.
Adult basic skills	A category of education, typically below high school level and offered noncredit, to assist adults with low ability or training in reading, writing, or mathematics.
Boot camp	A short-term intensive experience designed for quick results. Colleges may offer, for example, a math boot camp designed to bring students up to college-level math skills during a 2-week period prior to the beginning of the semester.
Bridge program	Prematriculation programs generally conducted during the summer prior to college enrollment designed to improve academic skills and create a network of support structures.
College ready	A popular term to identify incoming college students who have scored high enough on placement tests to preclude the need for developmental courses.
Compression	A course or curricular design that results in less time spent in developmental education. Compression may consist of combining or eliminating developmental course levels.
Cut scores	The lowest score on a test used for classification, or placement, or other purpose.
Developmental climb	The process of passing a developmental course and progressing to the next level.
Developmental education	Courses, typically in English, mathematics, or reading, with content below college level. Remedial and developmental are often used interchangeably. Other terms include compensatory and precollege.
ESL	English as a second language. Courses or programs designed to teach speakers of other languages to listen, read, write, and speak English.
GED	General Education Diploma. The GED is a test that determines if a person has the requisite skills and knowledge consistent with a high school graduate.
Learning community	Cohort-type of arrangement where students are purposely grouped within a set of courses and/or study groups.
Mainstreaming	The practice of allowing students who test below college level to concurrently enroll in developmental and college level courses.
Modularization	A curricular practice that decouples developmental instruction from the course structure. Modules are curricular segments that are presented to students dependent on their individual deficits.
Placement tests	Tests designed to determine an appropriate level of courses for enrollment.

LINDA HAGEDORN is professor and associate dean of the College of Human Sciences at Iowa State University.

INNA KUZNETSOVA is a graduate student within the School of Education at Iowa State University.

This chapter describes the establishment of the Minority Male Community College Collaborative (M2C3), a research and practice center at San Diego State University. M2C3 partners with community colleges across the United States to enhance access, achievement, and success among men of color. This chapter begins with a description of the national trends and concerns that led to the center's focus on supporting the capacity of community colleges to address challenges facing historically underrepresented and underserved men, particularly men of color. Next, the chapter describes the concepts of "equity-mindedness" and "institutional responsibility" that informed the conceptualization of the center's intervention approach. Guided by these concepts, partnerships advanced by institutional assessment tools such as the Community College Survey of Men (CCSM), the Community College Insights Protocol (CCIP), and the Community College Student Success Inventory (CCSSI) are described.

Establishing a Research Center: The Minority Male Community College Collaborative (M2C3)

J. Luke Wood, Marissa Vasquez Urias, Frank Harris III

In Fall 2011, the Minority Male Community College Collaborative (M2C3) was established at San Diego State University's Interwork Institute. M2C3 is a national research and practice center that partners with community colleges to enhance their capacity to support the success of historically underserved men, particularly men of color. Since its founding, the center has partnered with over 100 community colleges across the nation. This chapter describes the establishment and functions of M2C3, beginning with a description of the national trends and concerns that led to the center's development. Also described is the epistemological perspectives employed by M2C3 to support institutional research professionals in gathering inquiry-driven evidence that promote equity mindedness and institutional responsibility.

New Directions for Institutional Research, no. 168 © 2016 Wiley Periodicals, Inc.
Published online in Wiley Online Library (wileyonlinelibrary.com) • DOI: 10.1002/ir.20161

The Rationale for a National Center

There are numerous factors that led to the creation of M2C3. Chief among these were (a) glaring outcome disparities between men of color and their peers, (b) limited research on community college men, (c) ineffective practices shaped by perspectives from the literature on 4-year institutions, (d) a lack of attentiveness to non-Black men of color, (e) inadequate employment of assessment for interventions targeting men of color, and (f) inadequate attention on the role of identity in student success.

Across the nation, scholars and practitioners are increasingly concerned about outcome disparities between men of color and their peers. With the use of data from the Beginning Postsecondary Students Longitudinal study, Wood, Harris, and Xiong (2014) found that only 17.1% of Black men and 15.4% of Latino men earned a certificate or degree, or transferred from a community college to a 4-year institution within a 3-year time frame as compared to 27% of White men. In addition, Wood and colleagues found variances by full- and part-time enrollment. Although 38.6% of full-time White men completed their goals in 3 years, only 26.1% of Black and 20.3% of Latino men did so. Similar patterns are evident for mixed (full and part time) enrollment students. Among these, 15% of Black and 15.2% of Latino men achieved their goals in 3 years, the rate nearly doubled for White men at 29.7%. Subsequent scholarship has found that Pacific Islander, Native American, and Southeast Asian (e.g., Hmong, Cambodian, Laotian, Vietnamese) men have experiences and outcomes on par with Black and Latino men (Wood & Harris, 2014; Wood, Harris, & Mazyck, 2015).

When M2C3 was founded in 2011, research specific to men of color in community colleges was woefully lacking. Although barriers to the success of boys and men of color in education had been rigorously explicated by scholars (Allen, 1986; Cuyjet, 1997, 2006; Davis, 2003; Davis & Palmer, 2010; Harper, Carini, Bridges, & Hayek, 2004; Palmer, Davis, & Hilton, 2009), the vast majority was focused on Black boys in K–12 education, Black men in historically Black colleges and universities, and Black high-achieving and gifted males (Wood & Palmer, 2014). In fact, although hundreds of studies had been published on males of color in education, only a handful had focused on the community college context (Wood & Hilton, 2012). This was concerning, given that community colleges serve as the primary pathway into postsecondary education for men of color (Wood, Palmer, & Harris, 2015). Moreover, the literature on men of color focused almost exclusively on Black males, overlooking other historically underrepresented populations including Latino, Native American, Pacific Islander, and Southeast Asian men. Thus, the educational realities of these men lacked appropriate understanding.

Given the national void of literature on men of color in the community college, research and policy efforts were generally guided by the 4-year literature base on these men. However, there are significant differences between men of color in community colleges and 4-year institutions that severely inhibit the utility of 4-year college research and theories (Wood, 2011). Black men in community colleges are more likely to be older, have dependents, be independent, and have delayed enrollment into postsecondary education. They are less likely to have higher degree aspirations or to have completed high school coursework in foreign language, mathematics, and science. These differences led Wood (2013) to assert that Black men in community colleges are "the same, but different" from their 4-year counterparts. As such, the application of research on 4-year collegiate men to community college men is a core barrier to the success of male initiatives in community colleges (Wood, 2013).

In addition to the challenges of applicability, these initiatives often lacked in adequate assessment, evaluation, and institutional support. Many efforts lack data to inform the programmatic designs or to demonstrate greater outcomes for their target populations beyond anecdotal stories from a handful of men (Wood & Harris, 2015a). Programs are often eliminated because it is difficult to establish and/or align program and student learning outcomes with data demonstrating their effectiveness (Wood & Harris, 2015a). In addition to gathering program-level data, some campuses lack institutional buy-in and support (Wood & Harris, 2015b) from campus leaders. As such, key stakeholders did not prioritize opportunities for collaboration between program staff and institutional research offices, resulting in a lack of program needs- or outcomes-based assessments (Wood & Harris, 2015a).

Furthermore, many campuses employing male initiatives did not account for the fact that men of color often have salient identities as men, which greatly influence their success in college (Harris, 2010; Sáenz, Bukoski, Lu, & Rodriguez, 2013; Wood & Harris, 2015a). The role of men as breadwinners, their apprehension to seek help, perceptions of competition and achievement, as well as views of school as a domain more suited for the success of women than men, greatly affect outcomes for college men of color (Harris & Harper, 2008). Also of critical importance, efforts designed to enhance success for community college men of color were *solely* student focused. Campuses employed mentoring programs and life-skills workshops, efforts that are notoriously difficult to scale (Wood & Harris, 2015a). Campuses typically did little, if anything, to build the capacity of faculty, advisors, tutors, and other staff to educate men of color (Wood & Harris, 2015b). As a result, the focus of these interventions reinforced a perspective among educators that students were solely to blame for outcome disparities.

M2C3 was established given the issues facing research and practices for community college men of color. In the next section, we delineate the epistemological orientation informing the M2C3 intervention design.

Epistemological Foundations of M2C3

M2C3's research and practice design is informed by the work of Dr. Estela Mara Bensimon. Bensimon is Professor of Higher Education and Co-Director of the Center for Urban Education (CUE) at the University of Southern California. Her research addresses racial inequities in postsecondary education through the perspective of organizational learning. In this vein, CUE partners with colleges and universities to use data, benchmarking, and inquiry processes to highlight and redress identified disparities. Frank Harris III, prior to serving as the founding Co-Director of M2C3, served as the Associate Director of CUE under Bensimon. This experience served to shape the core epistemological foundations of M2C3.

To inculcate equity perspectives among educational scholars, Bensimon established the Equity and Critical Policy Institutes. The Institutes sought to train emerging scholars from the Association for the Study of Higher Education (ASHE) on how to reorient quantitative qualitative and policy research to address educational equity. Both Harris and Wood participated in several of these Institutes, providing them with formalized training in the concepts of equity-mindedness and institutional responsibility.

Equity-mindedness is a "multi-dimensional theoretical construct derived from concepts of fairness, social justice, and human agency … [by] achieving equal educational outcomes for college students from racial and ethnic groups that have a history of enslavement, colonization, or oppression" (Bensimon, Rueda, Dowd, & Harris, 2007, p. 32). Educators who are equity-minded recognize practices that are exclusionary, and are aware of institutional racism and how power inequities produce disparate outcomes for students (Bensimon, 2007). Guided by this awareness, equity-minded scholars assume that the origin of disparate outcomes is primarily constructed by institutional breakdowns rather than student deficiencies. As such, equity-minded scholars are informed by the concept of institutional responsibility, where educators take ownership for inequities and concentrate on factors within their power to counter institutional deficits. Notions of equity-mindedness and institutional responsibility chiefly inform the functions of M2C3.

Given the focus on institutional responsibility as informed by organizational learning, M2C3 has also adopted a systems-theory perspective. Guided by the words of W. Edward Deming, who suggested that, "every system is perfectly designed to achieve the results that it gets," M2C3 aims to support educators, leaders, and institutional researchers in applying this notion to their specific contexts. M2C3 regularly highlights this quote, asking individuals to consider how every system, every college, every department, and every classroom are perfectly designed to achieve the results they get.

Functions of M2C3

M2C3 was established with the vision of becoming the national hub for research and practice focused on historically underrepresented and underserved men in community colleges. Guided by this vision, the M2C3 Co-Directors sought insights from highly regarded national scholars who could shed light on how to establish a research center. Many conversations involved how to obtain fiscal viability to operate a center. One national scholar recommended a funding model that avoided reliance on grant resources. This model included arranging direct service contracts with institutions, which would allow for greater focus on their individual needs.

Much discussion also focused on the name of M2C3, the Minority Male Community College Collaborative. In general, scholars have shifted away from the use of the term *minority*, which can serve to "other" and diminish the importance of communities of color. However, within the community college context, most programs and initiatives serving men of color were called minority male initiatives (MMIs). As a result, M2C3 was named with the intent of communicating to MMI leaders that M2C3 was created to serve their needs. The "mission of the collaborative is to develop knowledge and advance promising practices that enhance access, achievement and success among men who have been historically underrepresented and underserved in postsecondary education" (Minority Male Community College Collaborative, 2015). Three primary functions—assessment, capacity development, and research—were organized around this mission.

Assessment

The focus of M2C3's assessment and evaluation agenda is informed by the data versus inquiry paradigm espoused by Bensimon. Under the data paradigm, institutional researchers are tasked with collecting disaggregated data that reveal equity gaps between students of color and their peers. Such findings then prompt college leaders and other stakeholders to engage solutions that are based upon the research literature or what has taken place in other locales. Yet, given the limitations of the research agenda on community college men of color, the data paradigm inhibits the ability of institutional leaders to advance outcomes for these male collegians.

Juxtaposed to the data paradigm, Bensimon argues that colleges should engage an inquiry paradigm. In this paradigm, interventions are informed by institutional-level data that provide insight into the equity gaps specific to the campus. Inquiry can be multifaceted in nature, comprised interviews, focus groups, surveys, self-assessments, and other data sources that encompass all institutional actors (e.g., students, faculty, and staff). Based upon these data, college leaders can then engage in meaningful dialogue about designing solutions to address equity gaps unique to the socio-cultural-political context of their campus. Further, evaluation of the inquiry-informed solutions is necessary to determine effectiveness, as well as to identify areas of improvement.

M2C3 has created a litany of instruments designed to inform the development of interventions for men of color and to assess their effectiveness. Chief among these instruments is the Community College Survey of Men (CCSM), recently renamed the Community College Success Measure (still the CCSM). This instrument is an institutional-level needs assessment tool that identifies factors influencing the success of college men of color. The CCSM design was informed by the published research on college men (e.g., Dancy & Brown, 2012; Harper & Harris, 2010, 2012; Harris, 2010; Harris & Harper, 2008; Palmer & Strayhorn, 2008; Sáenz & Ponjuan, 2011) and more specifically, the research literature on community college men of color (e.g., Bush & Bush, 2005, 2010; Sáenz et al., 2013; Wood, 2012a, 2012b, 2012c; Wood & Essien-Wood, 2012; Wood, Hilton, & Lewis, 2011).

The CCSM is administered in randomly selected classes with an oversampling of developmental education courses where men of color are often concentrated. Partnering colleges receive a report that includes descriptive statistics, within-group analyses, and predictive analytics. Within-group analyses consist of a presentation of the CCSM's items and scales based on predetermined thresholds of being acceptable, concerning, or an area of immediate intervention. These classifications were derived from threshold scores established from prior inquiry across 60 community colleges with the use of data from 12,000 men. Thresholds termed *acceptable* represent instances where less than 20% of respondents indicate a level of dissatisfaction or frequency of "never" across response categories. Instances greater than 20% are termed *concerning*, and those indicating 30% or above are termed *area of immediate intervention*. The final section of the report includes predictive analyses that model faculty items and scales on faculty–student interactions; noncognitive outcomes on students' action control (i.e., focus in school); and student services factors on their use of services on campus.

An extensive amount of M2C3 efforts are dedicated to assessing and enhancing the psychometric properties of the CCSM and other instruments. For instance, the CCSM was validated across a sample of 12,000 men in eight states, over 2 years, in three distinct phases. These activities are discussed further in the Research section. In addition to the CCSM, M2C3 has created other instruments, including (a) the Community College Student Success Inventory (CCSSI), an institutional self-assessment tool for determining an institution's readiness to facilitate successful outcomes for men of color; (b) the Male Program Assessment of College Excellence (M-PACE), an outcomes-based assessment tool for programs and initiatives serving men of color; (c) the Community College Insights Protocol (CCIP), a focus-group protocol for understanding the perceptions and experiences of students that shape their outcomes in college settings; and (d) the Community College Instructional Development Inventory

(CC-IDI), an institutional level inventory to inform professional development programming for instructional faculty who teach underserved students.

M2C3 assessment partnerships with colleges are intensive in nature, often involving quantitative and qualitative data collection, as well as intensive professional development activities based on the assessment results. Such partnerships serve to support often overburdened institutional research offices with the inquiry needed to guide equity-focused efforts. Meta-level insights gleaned from these activities also serve to inform the capacity development of M2C3, which is discussed in the next section.

Capacity Development

Supporting the capacity of community colleges to advance student success outcomes for men of color has been a principal objective of M2C3. Recognizing that few practitioners have the time to read peer-reviewed journal articles, we found it critical to provide information to college professionals in a manner that was flexible and accessible to them. As a result, M2C3 established a rigorous schedule of webinars that addresses an array of topics focused on men of color. The first webinar was hosted in April of 2014 and was titled, "Men of Color in the Community College: Trends, Challenges, and Opportunities." The webinar, attended by over 250 participants, resulted in an increased organizational focus on this communication medium. Between July 2014 and December of 2014, M2C3 hosted three more webinars, addressing (a) the design and implementation of minority male initiatives, (b) teaching and learning strategies for men of color, and (c) a session on how to use the Community College Student Success Inventory (CCSSI). Webinar participation quickly grew, averaging over 1,200 participants across 250 to 300 community college sites. Many community colleges began showing the webinars in large rooms filled with faculty and staff concerned about improving outcomes for men of color.

When M2C3 begin in 2011, the organization set out to actualize a national consortium focused on community college men. However, given the extensive time demands of validating instruments, the consortium was not formalized until February of 2015, when M2C3 launched the National Consortium on College Men of Color (NCCMC). The consortium was organized via a member-college design, in which colleges interested in innovative practices and policies for addressing the achievement of underrepresented men could join. Consortium colleges receive access to M2C3 webinars, participate in information-sharing sessions on promising practices, can engage in conversations on strategic equity efforts using the member-only virtual discussion board, and attend an annual working group meeting in San Diego, CA. At the working group, individuals participate in a 2-day program designed to engage cross-institutional conversations and prepare action plans for strategic equity efforts.

Several key national organizations and associations became partners with M2C3 in support of the NCCMC. These affiliates include Community College League of California (CCLC), League of Innovation in the Community College, American College Personnel Association (ACPA), Association of Community College Trustees (ACCT), National Association of Diversity Officers in Higher Education (NADOHE), and African American Male Education Network and Development (A2MEND). These partner organizations provide insight on prospective topics to be discussed during webinars and information-sharing sessions, participate in consortium activities, and help to expand the reach of the consortium. For example, ACPA has made all consortium webinar recordings available through the ACPA on-demand website, so that student affairs practitioners in colleges and universities can benefit from the content. All M2C3 partners have been integral to the success of the consortium and the expansion of the network of partner colleges.

Recognizing that some colleges were apprehensive about joining the consortium due to internal and local campus politics, the webinar series has remained free and open to all individuals who want to attend. Under the consortium banner, five webinars have taken place, addressing topics such as counseling and advising men of color, assessing initiatives serving men of color, using the M-PACE for outcome assessment, equity-based strategic planning, and narratives of men who successfully transferred from the community college. In addition, the NCCMC hosts webinars scheduled at least once a month on topics raised by member colleges and affiliate partners. Currently, there are 67 member colleges of the NCCMC. In addition, thousands of community college professionals participate in the webinar series, which now average participation of 600 to 650 college sites per webinar. Although capacity development activities are primarily advanced through the NCCMC, M2C3 also provides on-campus professional development training for issues relevant to men of color. Moreover, the M2C3 website houses a free virtual warehouse on scholarly publications that address men of color in community colleges. This includes links to books, peer-reviewed journal articles, book chapters, reports, popular press articles, and other key publications.

Research

As previously noted, prior to the founding of M2C3, only a handful of studies had been published on men of color in the community college. M2C3 has greatly expanded the literature base; now, there are 61 articles, books, book chapters, and reports accessible through the virtual warehouse. Of these, the majority (66%) have been written by M2C3 staff or students, whose research is primarily informed by the Socio-Ecological Outcomes (SEO) model, as articulated by Wood et al. (2014) and Wood, Harris, and White (2015).

The SEO model postulates that four interrelated domains influence the success of men of color in college; these are noncognitive, academic, environmental, and campus ethos outcomes. The noncognitive domain is comprised of two sets of factors: (a) intrapersonal factors that depict students' psychosocial outcomes (e.g., self-efficacy, degree utility, locus of control, action control, intrinsic interest) and (b) identity outcomes that focus on racial and gender identities (with a specific focus on breadwinner orientation, help-seeking, and perceptions of school as a feminine domain) as well as other salient identities (e.g., spiritual, sexual).

The academic domain is comprised factors commonly associated with campus involvement, including interactions with faculty and staff, as well as the use of student services. The environmental domain captures factors that occur outside of college that influence student success inside of college, including familial responsibility, transportation, employment, stressful life events, and similar considerations. The last domain, campus ethos, examines campus climate and culture, with a focus on validation from faculty and staff, perceptions of belonging from faculty, perceptions of being welcome to engage in and out of class, and other ethos factors. As articulated by Wood et al. (2015), the campus ethos and environmental domains are perceived as having an influence on the noncognitive and academic domains. A bidirectional relationship between the noncognitive and academic domains is also evident. Altogether, the interaction among these domains is perceived as having an influence on student success outcomes (e.g., persistence, achievement, attainment, transfer). This model has enabled the team to focus intently on the role of intrapersonal factors (e.g., self-efficacy, degree utility, locus of control), identity, and campus ethos on student success outcomes. Aggregate data from the CCSM and MPACE serve as apt sources for secondary research; however, large data sets such as the Beginning Postsecondary Students Longitudinal Study and Educational Longitudinal Study have also provided key insights.

Holistically, the M2C3 research agenda centers on factors that influence student success outcomes for men of color. The capacity development activities (particularly through the consortium) and assessment work of M2C3 often frame new research trajectories. This enables M2C3 to produce scholarship that informs practice and to enable practice that informs scholarship. The focus on men of color has been most intensive around Black, Latino, and Southeast Asian men (because of the research interests of individual team members). A number of M2C3 publications have also focused on evaluations of the psychometric properties of M2C3 assessment tools (e.g., De la Garza, Wood, & Harris, 2015; Harris & Wood, 2014; Wood & Harris, 2014). Prior to release, all M2C3 tools are rigorously validated for face, content, construct, predictive and confirmatory validity; and scale reliability. Given the focus on within-racial/ethnic group analyses, construct validity and scale reliability must be demonstrated for multiple racial/ethnic groups. As a result, validation efforts require an extensive dedication of time and resources, especially in consideration that most M2C3 instruments are given to colleges for use free of charge.

Although M2C3 is primarily staffed by faculty and graduate researchers, there is also great value and attention placed on the need to train the next generation of equity-minded scholars in education. Motivated by this notion, M2C3 operates the Aztec Research Fellowship Program (ARFP). The ARFP is an undergraduate fellowship program for students who are interested in researching issues relevant to men of color in community colleges. Most program fellows have formerly attended community colleges; all fellows attend SDSU. Fellows are fully integrated into the M2C3 research team, receiving coaching on methods of inquiry. At the end of each year, ARFP participants present their research at conferences and have opportunities to publish their results in peer-reviewed research journals. Advancing the next generation of scholars is critical to ensuring that the momentum gained within the past few years on college men of color continues to grow.

Concluding Remarks

In this chapter, the authors described the national trends and concerns that led to M2C3's focus on supporting the capacity of community colleges to address challenges facing historically underrepresented and underserved men, particularly men of color. The chapter also described the concepts of *equity-mindedness* and *institutional responsibility* that informed the conceptualization of the center's intervention approach. Guided by these concepts, an overview of the assessment, capacity-development, and research functions of M2C3 were described. Particular attention was given to M2C3 partnerships that are advanced by institutional assessment tools, such as the Community College Survey of Men (CCSM), the Community College Insights Protocol (CCIP), and the Community College Student Success Inventory (CCSSI). These tools enable M2C3 to understand better the complexity of challenges facing college men of color. Furthermore, M2C3 seeks to continue its collaborative efforts with partner colleges, whose campus leaders and institutional research offices play a critical role in facilitating equity-focused strategies to support male students of color in community college.

References

Allen, W. R. (1986). *Gender and campus race differences in Black student academic performance, racial attitudes and college satisfaction*. Atlanta, GA: Southern Education Foundation.

Bensimon, E. M. (2007). The underestimated significance of practitioner knowledge in the scholarship on student success. *Review of Higher Education*, *30*(4), 441–469.

Bensimon, E. M., Rueda, R., Dowd, A. C., & Harris, F., III (2007). Accountability, equity, and practitioner learning and change. *Metropolitan Universities*, *18*(3), 28–45.

Bush, E. C., & Bush, L. (2005). Black male achievement and the community college. *Black Issues in Higher Education*, *22*(2), 44.
Bush, E. C., & Bush, L. (2010). Calling out the elephant: An examination of African American male achievement in the community colleges. *Journal of African American Males in Education*, *1*(1), 40–62.
Cuyjet, M. J. (Ed.). (1997). Helping African American men succeed in college. *New Directions for Student Services, 80*.
Cuyjet, M. J. (Ed.). (2006). *African American men in college*. San Francisco, CA: Jossey-Bass
Dancy, T. E., & Brown, M. C. (2012). *African American males and education: Researching the convergence of race and identity*. Charlotte, NC: Information Age
Davis, J. E. (2003). Early schooling and academic achievement of African American males. *Urban Education*, *38*(5), 515–537.
Davis, R. J., & Palmer, R. T. (2010). The role and relevancy of postsecondary remediation for African American students: A review of research. *Journal of Negro Education*, *79*(4), 503–520.
De la Garza, T., Wood, J. L., & Harris, F. III. (2015). An exploratory assessment of the validity of the Community College Survey of Men (CCSM): Implications for serving veteran men. *Community College Journal of Research and Practice*, *39*(3), 293–298.
Harper, S. R., Carini, R. M., Bridges, B. K., & Hayek, J. (2004). Gender differences in student engagement among African American undergraduates at historically Black colleges and universities. *Journal of College Student Development*, *45*(3), 271–284.
Harper, S. R., & Harris, F., III (Eds.). (2010). *College men and masculinities: Theory, research, and implications for practice*. San Francisco, CA: Jossey-Bass.
Harper, S. R., & Harris, F., III. (2012). *A role for policymakers in improving the status of Black male students in U.S. higher education*. Washington, DC: Institute for Higher Education Policy.
Harris, F., III. (2010). College men's conceptualizations of masculinities and contextual influences: Toward a conceptual model. *Journal of College Student Development*, *51*(3), 297–318.
Harris, F., III, & Harper, S. R. (2008). Masculinities go to community college: Understanding male identity socialization and gender role conflict. *New Directions for Community Colleges*, *142*, 25–35.
Harris, F., III, & Wood, J. L. (2014). Community college student success inventory (CC-SSI) for men of color in community colleges: Content validation summary. *Community College Journal of Research and Practice*, *38*(12), 1185–1192.
Minority Male Community College Collaborative. (2015). *About us*. Retrieved from http://interwork.sdsu.edu/sp/m2c3/about-us/
Palmer, R. T., Davis, R. J., & Hilton, A. A. (2009). Exploring challenges that threaten to impede the academic success of academically underprepared African American male collegians at an HBCU. *Journal of College Student Development*, *50*(4), 429–445.
Palmer, R. T., & Strayhorn, T. L. (2008). Mastering one's own fate: Non-cognitive factors with the success of African American males at an HBCU. *National Association of Student Affairs Professionals Journal*, *11*(1), 126–143.
Sáenz, V. B., Bukoski, B. E., Lu, C., & Rodriguez, S. (2013). Latino males in Texas community colleges: A phenomenological study of masculinity constructs and their effect on college experiences. *Journal of African American Males in Education*, *4*(2), 5–24.
Sáenz, V. B., & Ponjuan, L. (2011). *Men of color: Ensuring academic success for Latino males in higher education*. Washington, DC: Institute for Higher Education Policy.
Wood, J. L. (2011, August 5). Developing successful Black male initiatives. *Community College Times*. Retrieved from: http://www.ccdaily.com/Pages/Opinions/Developing-successful-black-male-programs-and-initiatives.aspx

Wood, J. L. (2012a). Black males in the community college: Using two national datasets to examine academic and social integration. *Journal of Black Masculinity*, *2*(2), 56–88.

Wood, J. L. (2012b). Examining academic variables effecting the persistence and attainment of Black male collegians: A focus on performance and integration in the community college. *Race Ethnicity and Education*, *17*(5), 601–622.

Wood, J. L. (2012c). Leaving the two-year college: Predictors of black male collegian departure. *The Journal of Black Studies*, *43*(3), 303–326.

Wood, J. L. (2013). The same … but different: Examining background characteristics among Black males in public two year colleges. *Journal of Negro Education*, *82*(1), 47–61.

Wood, J. L., & Essien-Wood, I. R. (2012). Capital identity projection: Understanding the psychosocial effects of capitalism on Black male community college students. *Journal of Economic Psychology* *33*(3), 984–995.

Wood, J. L., & Harris, F., III. (2014). *Picturing inequity: An infographic report on persistence and completion for men in the California community college. Contributions from the African American Male Education Network and Development (A2MEND) and the Minority Male Community College Collaborative*. San Diego, CA: Minority Male Community College Collaborative.

Wood, J. L., & Harris, F., III. (2015a, May 5). Male program assessment for college excellence (MPACE) [Webinar]. In Webinars on Men of Color. Retrieved from https://www.youtube.com/watch?v=xA2sonYzGpU&feature=youtu.be

Wood, J. L., & Harris, F., III. (2015b, September 9). Men of color advocacy: How to gain institutional buy-in and support from institutional leaders [Webinar]. In Webinars on Men of Color. Retrieved from http://interwork.sdsu.edu/sp/m2c3/2015/09/09/register-now-free-webinar-on-gaining-institutional-buy-in-for-men-of-color-efforts/

Wood, J. L., & Harris, F., III, & Mazyck, J. (2015). *Picturing inequity: An infographic report on remediation in California community colleges*. San Diego, CA: Minority Male Community College Collaborative.

Wood, J. L., Harris, F., III, & White, K. (2015). *Teaching men of color in the community college: A guidebook*. San Diego, CA: Montezuma.

Wood, J. L., Harris, F., III, & Xiong, S. (2014). Advancing the success of men of color in the community college: Special issue on the Community College Survey of Men. *Journal of Progressive Policy and Practice*, 2(2), 129–133.

Wood, J. L., & Hilton, A. A. (2012). A meta-synthesis of literature on Black males in the community college: An overview on nearly forty years of policy recommendations. In A. A. Hilton, J. L. Wood, & C. W. Lewis (Eds.), *Black Males in postsecondary education: Examining their experiences in diverse institutional contexts* (pp. 5–27). Charlotte, NC: Information Age.

Wood, J. L., Hilton, A. A., & Lewis, C. (2011). Black male collegians in public two-year colleges: Student perspectives on the effect of employment on academic success. *National Association of Student Affairs Professionals Journal*, *14*(1), 97–110.

Wood, J. L., & Palmer, R. T. (2014). *Black male students in higher education: A guide to ensuring success*. New York, NY: Routledge.

Wood, J. L., Palmer, R. T., & Harris, F. III (2015). Men of color in community colleges: A synthesis of empirical findings. In M. B. Paulsen (Ed.), *Higher education: Handbook of theory and research*. New York, NY: Springer International.

J. LUKE WOOD *is associate professor of Community College Leadership and the Director of the Doctoral Program Concentration in Community College Leadership at San Diego State University (SDSU).*

MARISSA VASQUEZ URIAS *is an assistant professor of Postsecondary Education and Community College Leadership at San Diego State University. She also serves as the Associate Director of the Minority Male Community College Collaborative (M2C3).*

FRANK HARRIS III *is an associate professor of Postsecondary Education and the Co-Director of the Minority Male Community College Collaborative (M2C3) at San Diego State University.*

5

Graduate programs in higher education administration and leadership have sought to equip students with the knowledge, skills, and competencies for higher education leadership; that is, to prepare globally minded leaders who can navigate the internal and external demands of, and for, higher education. With the use of the Lattuca and Stark model of curriculum as an academic plan, this chapter provides an overview of opportunities and challenges to be considered when developing higher education leadership graduate programs.

Higher Education Leadership Graduate Program Development

Sydney Freeman, Jr., Crystal Renée Chambers, Rochelle Newton

Worldwide there are over 15,000 institutions of higher education, of which just over 9,000 are universities (Hazelkorn, 2011). The number of institutions notwithstanding, student learning and development is a global challenge. The Organization for Economic Cooperation and Development (OECD) (2015) reports that although there are more individuals receiving a higher education, literacy and numeracy skills among the populous have not concomitantly improved. Countries such as Italy, Spain, and the United States have higher proportions of citizens with college degrees, but in terms of skills, they rank alongside Japanese high school graduates. The greatest gains in the number of participants in higher education are made in emergent nations such as Argentina, India, Saudi Arabia, and South Africa. This is especially true when it comes to the science, technology, engineering, and mathematics (STEM) fields. Yet when considering the imbalance among Western nations in the talent pool of individuals with STEM degrees, one of many challenges facing higher education globally, responses tend to be local (Branković, Klemenčič, Lažetić, & Zgaga, 2014).

Wright (2007) suggests that any sector as large as higher education should be systematically studied, analyzed, and evaluated, and the data gleaned therefrom applied to the management, direction, and leadership. She goes on to state, "The responsibility for operating colleges and universities is greater than ever: No longer can its leadership roles be filled by amateurs" (p. 22). Toward this end, graduate programs in higher education administration and leadership seek to equip students with the knowledge, skills, and competencies for higher education leadership; that is, to produce globally minded leaders who can navigate the internal and external demands of, and for, higher education. In this chapter, we use the Lattuca and Stark (2009) model of curriculum as an academic plan to connect strategic and academic planning.

Strategic and Academic Planning at the University Level

In *Academic Strategy*, Keller (1983) predicted the closure or merger of up to 30% of higher education institutions in the United States by 1995 if colleges and universities failed to plan for fundamental shifts to the business of higher education:

> . . . higher education in the United States has entered a revolutionary period, one in which not only the finances and number of students are changing sharply but also the composition of the entire clientele, the kinds of courses and programs wanted and schedules for them, the degree of competitiveness among colleges, the technology needed on campus, the nature of the faculty, and the growing extent of external control and regulations. (pp. 25–26)

Fortunately, Keller's prediction did not materialize; yet conditions undergirding his predictions seem metastasized, especially since the Great Recession of 2008. The field of higher education faces pressures inside and out to improve fiscal efficiencies, increase revenues from nongovernmental sources, decrease expenditures, and grow, improving reputation, quality, marketing, and outreach to an increasingly diverse and consumeristic student base (Dickeson, 2010). Boyer (1990), and the Spellings Commission (2006) lambasted institutions of higher education for their inability to demonstrate quality in student learning outcomes in spite of escalating costs of college degrees. The inability of institutions of higher education to produce measurable results painted higher education leaders as aloof and unaccountable (Middaugh, 2009). Keller's (1983) advice was that institutions "construct a more active, change-oriented management style" and declared, "the era of laissez-faire campus administration is over" (p. 26). If Keller's observations were not obvious then, they are today.

As observed by Morrill (2010), Keller's call to strategic action in the 1980s resulted in a shift in decision making in higher education from short-term, ad hoc approaches to long-term vision and goal orientation. Although we in academe may be more used to hearing the terminology of strategy and planning, there still exists broad resistance as the tenor of academic planning often is equated with managerialism. Yet, without clear vision of what we want or strategy, anything goes.

Amid contemporary fiscal and resource constraints, the luxury of emergent academic planning is not feasible for most institutions. As most academic programs are "seriously undernourished," unplanned growth is unsustainable (Dickeson, 2010, p. 23). Academic planning is the heart and soul of an institution's overall strategic plan, and as such, academic and institutional plans should be developed concomitantly, informing and being informed by each other (Sherman & Rowley, 2004).

Toward this end, academic planning should begin with a well-defined institutional mission (Middaugh, 2009). The role of leadership here is "mobilizing commitment to shared purposes and goals" (Morrill, 2010, p. 135). A discussion of mission development is beyond the scope of the present paper (but see Morrill, 2010; Sheehan, 2010; Taylor, 2013). Instead, what we want to emphasize is the placement of academic planning within the larger institutional strategic planning context. Here, "not only must mission and vision set an authentic direction that connects with the narrative of identity, but it must also develop the mechanisms through which the organization can attain its goals" (Morrill, 2010, p. 135). Academic planning within a larger institutional strategic plan and aligned with a well-defined mission will include consideration of external pressures and supports, internal assets, and alignment with the institution's overall market niche (Banta & Palomba, 2014; Kuh et al., 2015; Middaugh, 2009). This is discussed further in Chapter 2 relative to the creation of distinctive degrees, and illustrated in Chapter 7.

Lattuca and Stark (2009) enunciate a method of academic planning at the level of curriculum development.The academic plan is contextually influenced by external forces including the market, multiple levels of government, accrediting bodies, and disciplinary organizations. Internally, academic plans are (should be) shaped at the macro level by institutional mission, academic and support resources, and governance. At the unit level, there are considerations of content knowledge and norms, faculty expertise, and student characteristics.

We use this framework to discuss academic planning within the field of higher education leadership. Lattuca and Stark (2009) proffer eight elements of academic planning: (a) purpose, (b) content, (c) sequence, (d) learners, (e) instructional processes, (f) instructional resources, (g) evaluation, and (h) adjustment. Effective implementation and assessment strategies should be considered amid discussions of mission alignment, curricular content (including sequencing), students as learners, faculty expertise, workload, and departmental human and operational resources (Middaugh, 2009; Rothwell & Cookson, 1997).

Throughout the academic planning process, offices of institutional research can be of assistance through consulting on the overall academic program planning and analyses assessing a program's applicant pool, program trends in the areas of enrollment, retention, program completion, funding, assessments of faculty–student ratios, and course and program evaluation, among other activities. For programs in higher education as a field of study particularly, institutional research offices can provide quality internships, given their unique position overseeing all university units.

Graduate Program Development in Higher Education as a Field of Study

When thinking about graduate programs in higher education as a field of study, the direction and purposes of a program should directly align with overall institutional mission. After all, higher education programs are purposed to educate scholarly practitioners, researchers, and faculty experts (Card & Chambers, 2009; Townsend, 1990). Hence, developing high-quality educational programs is central to the advancement of academe (Hendricks, 2001; Townsend, 1990).

Purpose. Programmatic purpose derives from the knowledge, skills, and dispositions to be acquired over a course of study (Lattuca & Stark, 2009). According to Wright (2007), higher education graduate programs should equip students with the knowledge, skills, and competencies needed to do well in any career in higher education, whether in administrator, faculty, or policy roles. The three general areas of practice are college administration or leadership, student affairs and services, and college teaching. These areas can be practiced across institutional types—2- and 4-year contexts, for profit and not for profit, public and private. Most students arriving in a higher education graduate program often serve in a professional setting and are looking to advance in their careers, make a career change, or enhance their skills for marketability (Wright, 2007). Common reasons students pursue graduate education are a desire to learn more about their practice, personal satisfaction, improved job prospects, and needing an advanced degree for career progression (Malaney, 1987). These factors should be considered within the context of academic planning.

Content, Sequence, and Instructional Processes. Course content involves subject matters, delivered through and/or across coursework and paracurricular activities such as dissertations, theses, other graduate student research, conference presentations, and the like (Lattuca & Stark, 2009). Within the field of higher education administration and leadership, there are core curricula found across graduate degree programs: history of higher education and organizational leadership. Across Ed.D. programs, generally aimed toward the preparation of higher education practitioners, and Ph.D. programs, aimed toward the preparation of researcher scholars, a knowledge of law and finance are of increasing importance as stand-alone courses. Areas embedded across program types include governance, philosophy, and multiculturalism (Card, Chambers, & Freeman, in press; see also Bray, 2007 and Crosson & Nelson, 1986).

Course sequencing influences how students make sense of course content throughout the program of study (Lattuca & Stark, 2009). Arranging coursework logically (whether chronologically, thematically, or otherwise) helps students see connections between and among courses (Beebe, Mottet, & Roach, 2012). Faculty conversations about course sequence should center on educational benefits, but still attend to instructor concerns (Lattuca & Stark, 2009).

In terms of instructional processes, traditional course formats have not changed much since the early twentieth century (Cohen, 1988; Olds, 2008). There is an increasing number of instructional resources from which to choose—textbooks, e-books, YouTube, and publisher media options; classroom space with smart boards and global connectivity; laboratory, practicum, and internships. Given this particular field, incorporation of students' outside work and community experiences can add to the community of knowledge. Blending formal coursework with practical field experiences, fostering a healthy sense of praxis—merger of theory with practice—is ideal in this field of study (Freeman & Kochan, 2014), although the range of course tools should be considered (Lattuca & Stark, 2009).

Some instructional structures are more fixed. For example, course schedules are typically one to several times per week for 12–16 weeks. There is little evidence to support this scheduling over alternatives. Even in an age where technological advances revolutionize the "business of doing business," the legacy of these traditional formats lives in the online environment, including massive open online courses (MOOCS): New wine in old wine skins (Rees, 2014). That said, considering the needs and technological expertise (or lack thereof) of adult students, all technological innovations may not be appropriate. One of the authors of the present work recalls a discussion with a 50-year-old MBA student who, as part of his online program, had to create an avatar and access coursework via Second Life. The student had to ask his adolescent son for assistance with the task, a task the father perceived as not germane to his future work or field of study. This anecdote is illustrative of the tensions between innovation and student technological comfort and savvy. In planning course activities and delivery modes (online, distance, hybrid, MOOC), planners can accommodate the knowledge, skills, and abilities (KSAs) and multifaceted demands of adult learners.

Learners. Successful entry and completion of graduate programs are linked to the motivation and expectations of the students (Hawley, 1993; Rossman, 1995; Wlodkowski, 1993). Two decades of research in cognitive psychology, neuroscience, and biology all attest to the advantage of learner-centered teaching models over instructor-centered teaching models, at least for the students. Students learn more when the curriculum revolves around them, as opposed to the convenience and traditions of faculty (Doyle, 2011; Huba & Freed, 2000). Indeed, as learning should be the principal outcome of a curricular plan ". . . whether a curriculum 'works' may depend on whether the plan adequately accounts for students' goals and needs and addresses students' preparation and ability" (Lattuca & Stark, 2009, p. 10).

A firm understanding of expectations for entrance to graduate study is an important planning element. For most graduate-level entrance exams, there are no psychometric data available for adult learners, defined as persons ages 30 and up (for graduate students) and/or those whose last student experiences were a decade or more ago. At the lower end, these tests communicate basic literacy and at the higher end, although the tests may indicate quality academic experiences and ability, they do not account for noncognitive factors such as student effort (Donovan, 2013; Orlando, 2005; Sealey-Ruiz, 2012). Alternative admissions assessments such as interviews and impromptu writing samples can help in the admissions process.

Adult learners come to higher education graduate studies with a diverse set of needs and skills. Strong orientation programs, immersing students in contemporary technologies and library skills, alongside advising and mentorship, can improve the learning process for adult students (Robinson, 1999; Witte & Wolf, 2003; Wright, 2007).

Adult learners also have diverse sets of expectations. Ivankova and Stick (2005) identify three broad groups of students attracted to these programs: those who are mature, talented, and desire to earn their credential; those who are talented and eager, but lack the maturity to handle the pressure of program rigor; and those who seek to gain credentials while expending minimal effort. Given these divergent student types, program expectations should be articulated during the admissions process and reinforced through the course of study (Groccia, 1997). Student satisfaction is most closely linked to faculty success in meeting student expectations. In this vein, clearly communicating and reinforcing expectations can facilitate both student success and student reviews of faculty teaching (Lattuca & Stark, 2009).

Instructional Resources: Faculty Expertise, Workload, and Fiscal Support. Faculty expertise is a core academic planning consideration. Lattuca and Stark (2009) specifically advise against creating new programs or revising/expanding existing programs in areas where faculty expertise is insufficient. It is difficult to predict, and therefore plan for, additional faculty lines. At the outset, planners should ensure that they have or are able to attract and retain the right faculty (Olds, 2008; Patton, 2007). Professional development, such as the Council for the Advancement of Higher Education Programs' (CAHEP) Early Career Workshop, can help new and experienced faculty with curricular content and instructional strategies.

An additional consideration is faculty workload, and keeping faculty workloads competitive is important to retain a quality workforce. Teaching loads are just one consideration in addition to thesis and dissertation supervision, research, extramural funding, and institutional and community service (Middaugh, 2009). Graduate programs in higher education may require mentoring and internship experiences that are time-intensive elements for faculty (Witte & Wolf, 2003; Wright, 2007). At minimum, masters programs should employ at least two full-time tenure/tenure-track faculty, and doctoral programs should have three. Ideally, the program should hire a diverse core of full-time faculty educated with expertise in higher education core curriculum, using practitioners to augment faculty expertise (Bush et al., 2010). Related to workload, student credit hour generation is important for sustainability. Programs should aim to strike a balance between class sizes that permit the individualized attention expected in graduate programs and student credit hour production functions that keep programs safe from low productivity labels.

Department- and college-level leadership is necessary in securing and maintaining levels of human and fiscal resource support. Resource commitments should be clear (Uzoigwe, 1982) and planners should endeavor to develop positive working relationships with the department chair and other administrators (Kochan, 2010). It is important for programs to show themselves to be good departmental citizens, as very few higher education programs are standalone units (Western Michigan University, 2008–2009). An academic program cannot be divorced from the total department, college, or university culture (McKeachie & Svinicki, 2014).

Cultivating relationships with higher education leaders in the program's service area are important toward developing and sustaining a recruitment and collaborations network. Local politics will influence the way in which the program is approved, developed, and administered (Lattuca & Stark, 2009; McLean, 2000). Hence, academic planners should be sensitive to latent issues that may affect the planning, including institutional priorities, program alignment, and resource competition.

Evaluation and Adjustment. Evaluation and adjustment should be considered at the levels of individual students, courses, and program (Lattuca & Stark, 2009). At the student level, assessment information gives faculty insight into students' strengths to be fostered as well as areas for further development (Poda, 2007). Early assessments can help identify mismatches among student interests, abilities, career goals, and program emphases. Ongoing assessment provides opportunities to adjust and continually improve programming. For example, several graduate programs at East Carolina University employ an annual review of graduate students, accessing their academic skill development along Bloom's taxonomy. In addition to the faculty review component, this assessment includes opportunities for student self-reflection and communication of achievements. Students are a resource, as they can provide insights into what their needs are and can help assure program relevancy (Haynes, 1991; Mason, 1998; McLean, 2000).

Assessment at the course level encompasses student evaluations of instruction, peer evaluations, and expert evaluations (by individuals with an especial expertise in teaching, such as faculty affiliated with offices of faculty teaching excellence). Department and program internal and/or external peer evaluations typically accompany program-level review (Lattuca & Stark, 2009). To ensure assessments are objective, reliable, and fair (Olds, 2008), adjustments should be made for variances in signature pedagogies, instructional norms, and modalities across disciplines (Shulman, 2005). For higher education graduate programs, the Council for the Advancement of Higher Education Programs (CAHEP) has adopted programming guidelines at the masters' level, and is receiving comments on draft doctoral program guidelines (Bush et al., 2010; CAHEP, 2015).

Incorporating accrediting standards, competencies, or guidelines of regional and field specific agencies within their program design places an academic plan within a larger context, connecting to external constituencies in and outside of the university. Utilizing external guideposts reduces the level of individual faculty subjectivity in assessment and bolsters alignment with the field, discipline, and university. Cumulative, continuous, and relatively objective analysis provide a sound basis for program self-advocacy (Lattuca & Stark, 2009).

Conclusions and Implications for Practice

Higher education writ large continues to struggle with answers to the question of measurable value. As observed by Middaugh (2009, p. 6), criticisms of the academy have not been fully met by academe as "most colleges and universities lacked the quantitative and qualitative analytical evidence of institutional effectiveness." Those criticisms lodged at the institutional level translate to the program level for higher education administration and leadership graduate programs: What is it that educators in graduate programs of higher education leadership do to demonstrate they are preparing professionals to meet the challenges of higher education today? Academic planning concomitant with overall institutional strategic planning is smart for any academic discipline or field of study. However, the critiques of higher education leadership writ large especially hit our field of study. Toward that end, strategic academic planning is all the more imperative.

References

Banta, T., & Palomba, C. (2014). *Assessment essentials: Planning, implementing, and improving assessment in higher education.* San Francisco, CA: Jossey-Bass.

Beebe, S. A., Mottet, T. P., & Roach, K. D. (2012). *Training and development: Enhancing communication and leadership skills* (2nd ed.). Boston, MA: Allyn & Bacon.

Boyer, E. L. (1990). *Scholarship reconsidered: Priorities of the professoriate.* Princeton, NJ: Carnegie Foundation for the Advancement of Teaching.

Branković, J., Klemenčić, M., Lažetić, P., & Zgaga, P. (2014). *Global challenges, local responses in higher education: The contemporary issues in national and comparative perspective.* Rotterdam, The Netherlands: Sense Publishers.

Bray, N. J. (2007). Core curricula for American higher education. In D. Wright & M. Miller (Eds.), *Training higher education policy makers and leaders: A graduate program perspective* (pp. 111–121). Greenwich, CT: Information Age/Greenwood Publishing.

Bush, V. B. et al. (2010). *A commitment to quality: Guidelines for higher education administration and leadership preparation programs at the masters degree level. A proposal from the Executive Committee and the Ad Hoc Committee on Guidelines of the*

Council for the Advancement of Higher Education Programs. Retrieved from http://www.ashe.ws/images/CAHEPLeadershipProgramGuidelines.pdf

Card, K., & Chambers, C. (2009, November). *Core curricula in higher education programs: Becoming an academic discipline*. Paper presented to the Association for the Study of Higher Education, Council for the Advancement of Higher Education Programs, Jacksonville, FL.

Card, K., Chambers, C., & Freeman, S., Jr. (in press). Core curricula in higher education doctoral programs: Becoming a discipline. *International Journal of Doctoral Studies*.

Cohen, A. M. (1988). *The shaping of American higher education*. San Francisco, CA: Jossey-Bass.

Council for the Advancement of Higher Education (CAHEP). (2015). *A commitment to scanning quality and professional practice: Voluntary guidelines for higher education administration preparation programs at the doctoral degree level* (Working draft ed.). Las Vegas, NV: S. Freeman, Jr. & L. F. Goodchild.

Crosson, P., & Nelson, G. (1986). A profile of higher education doctoral program. *Review of Higher Education*, *93*, 335–357.

Dickeson, R. (2010). *Prioritizing academic programs and services: Reallocating resources to achieve strategic balance, revised and updated*. San Francisco, CA: Jossey-Bass.

Donovan, C. (2013). GRE unreliable predictor for graduate school acceptance. *The Blue Banner*. Retrieved from http://thebluebanner.net/gre-unreliable-predictor-for-graduate-school-acceptance/

Doyle, T. (2011). *Learner centered teaching: Putting research into action*. Sterling, VA: Stylus.

Freeman, S., Jr., & Kochan, F. (2014). Towards a theoretical framework for the doctorate in higher education administration. In S. Freeman, Jr., L. Hagedorn, L. Goodchild, & D. A. Wright (Eds.). *Advancing higher education as a field of study: In quest of doctoral degree guidelines—commemorating 120 years of excellence* (pp. 145–167). Sterling, VA: Stylus Publishing.

Groccia, J. E. (1997). The student as customer versus the student as learner. *About Campus*, *2*(2), 31–32.

Hawley, P. (1993). *Being bright is not enough: The unwritten rules of doctoral study*. Springfield, IL: Charles C. Thomas Publisher.

Haynes, L. J. (1991). Basic and knowledge and competency needs: Perspectives on the content needs of higher education administration programs. *Dissertation Abstracts International*, *A52–05*, 1654.

Hazelkorn, E. (2011). *Rankings and reshaping of higher education: The battle for world-class education*. Basingstoke, United Kingdom: Palgrave Macmillan.

Hendricks, S. (2001). Contextual individual factors and the use of influencing tactics in adult education program planning. *Adult Education Quarterly*, *51*(3), 219–235.

Huba, M. E., & Freed, J. E. (2000). *Learner-centered assessment on college campuses—Shifting the focus from teaching to learning*. Boston, MA: Allyn & Bacon.

Ivankova, N., & Stick, S. (2005, Fall). Preliminary model of doctoral students' persistence in the computer-mediated asynchronous learning environment. *Journal of Research in Education*, *15*(1), 123–144.

Keller, G. (1983). *Academic strategy: The management revolution in American higher education*. Baltimore, MD: The John Hopkins University Press

Kochan, F. (2010). Educational leadership redesign in Alabama: Deans' perspectives on organizational change. *Journal of Research on Leadership Education*, *5*(12), 507–530.

Kuh, G., Ikenberry, S., Jankowski, N., Cain, T., Ewell, P., Hutchings, P., & Kinzie, J. (2015). *Using evidence of student learning to improve higher education*. San Francisco, CA: Jossey-Bass.

Lattuca, L., & Stark, J. (2009). *Shaping the college curriculum: Academic plans in context*. San Francisco, CA: Jossey-Bass.

Malaney, G. D. (1987). Why students pursue graduate education, how they find out about a program, and why they apply to a specific school. *College and University, 62*(3), 247–258.

Mason, S. C. (1998). *A comparative analysis of the Doctor of Education and Doctor of Philosophy degrees in higher education: Expectations, curriculums and outcomes* (Doctoral dissertation). Available from Dissertations & Theses: A&I (Publication No. AAT 9826009).

McKeachie, W. J., & Svinicki, M. (2014). *Teaching tips: Strategies, research, and theory for college and university teachers* (14th ed.). Belmont, CA: Wadsworth.

McLean, S. (2000). Between rationality and politics: Autobiographical portraits of adult education programme planning. *International Journal of Lifelong Education, 19*(6), 493–505.

Middaugh, M. (2009). *Planning and assessment in higher education: Demonstrating institutional effectiveness.* San Francisco, CA: Jossey-Bass.

Morrill, R. (2010). *Strategic leadership: Integrating strategy and leadership in colleges and universities* (ACE Series on Higher Education). Lanham, MD: Rowman & Littlefield.

Olds, T. M. (2008). Colleges and universities. In J. Witte & M. Witte (Eds.), *Sources of adult education* (pp. 23–34). Dubuque, IA: Kendall/Hunt.

Organization for Economic Cooperation and Development. (OECD). (2015). *Education indicators in focus.* Retrieved from http://www.oecd.org/education/skills-beyond-school/EDIF%2031%20%282015%29—ENG—Final.pdf

Orlando, J. (2005). The reliability of GRE scores in predicting graduate school success: A meta-analytic, cross-functional, regressive, unilateral, post-Kantian, hyper-empirical, quadruple blind, verbiage-intensive and hemorrhoid-inducing study. *Ubiquity.* Retrieved from http://ubiquity.acm.org/article.cfm?id=1071921

Patton, C. (2007). Smart hiring: Facing future talent shortages, higher education institutions implement strategic staffing plans. *University Business, 10*(9), 25–27.

Poda, I. (2007). A framework for understanding assessment of student learning in higher education graduate programs. In D. Wright & M. Miller (Eds.), *Training higher education policy makers and leaders: A graduate program perspective* (pp. 111–121). Information Age/Greenwood Publishing Charlotte, NC

Rees, J. (2014). *More than MOOCs.* American Association of University Professors. Retrieved from http://www.aaup.org/article/more-moocs#.VXX1V89VhBc

Robinson, C. (1999). Developing a mentoring program: A graduate student's reflection of change. *Peabody Journal of Education, 74*(2), 119–134.

Rossman, M. H. (1995). *Negotiating graduate school.* Thousand Oaks, CA: Sage.

Rothwell, W., & Cookson, P. (1997). *Beyond instruction: Program planning in business and education.* San Francisco, CA: Jossey-Bass.

Sealey-Ruiz, Y. (2012). A way of making it: Black reentry females' success and challenges to undergraduate education. *National Journal of Urban Education and Practice, 5*(3), 363–375.

Sheehan, R. (2010). *Mission impact breakthrough strategies for nonprofits.* Hoboken, NJ: Jossey-Bass.

Sherman, H., & Rowley, D. (2004). *From strategy to change: Implementing the plan in higher education.* San Francisco, CA: Jossey-Bass.

Shulman, L. (2005). *Pedagogies of uncertainty.* Association of American Colleges & Universities. Retrieved from https://www.aacu.org/publications-research/periodicals/pedagogies-uncertainty

Spellings Commission. (2006). *A test of leadership: Charting the future of U.S. higher education.* Washington, DC: U.S. Department of Education.

Taylor, R. (2013). *The mission statement. A framework for developing an effective organizational mission statement in 100 words or less.* Venice Beach, CA: RT.

Townsend, B. (1990). Doctoral study in the field of higher education. In J. C. Smart (Ed.), *Higher education: Handbook of theory and research* (6th ed., pp. 161–200). New York, NY: Agathon Press.

Uzoigwe, C. N. (1982). *A model for establishing a higher education administration degree program at a Nigerian university* (Doctoral dissertation). Available from Dissertations & Theses: A&I (Publication No. AAT 8227819).

Western Michigan University. (2008–2009). *Model for institutional effectiveness and academic program planning*. Kalamazoo, MI: Author.

Witte, M., & Wolf, S. E. (2003). Infusing mentoring and technology within graduate courses: Reflections in practice. *Mentoring & Tutoring*, *11*(1), 95–103.

Wlodkowski, R. J. (1993). *Enhancing adult motivation to learn*. San Francisco, CA: Jossey-Bass.

Wright, D. (2007). Progress in the development of higher education as a specialized field of study. In D. Wright & M. Miller (Eds.), *Training higher education policymakers and leaders: A graduate perspective*. Charlotte, NC: Information Age Publishing.

SYDNEY FREEMAN, JR. is an associate professor of Higher Education Leadership at the University of Idaho.

CRYSTAL RENÉE CHAMBERS is an associate professor of Educational Leadership, Higher Education Concentration at East Carolina University.

ROCHELLE NEWTON is a manager of information technology at Duke University Law School and is a doctoral candidate in the Educational Leadership Program, Higher Education Concentration, at East Carolina University.

6

This chapter describes how data analysis and data-driven decision making were critical for designing, developing, and assessing a new academic program. The authors—one, the program's founder; the other, an alumna—begin by highlighting some of the elements in the program's incubation and, subsequently, describe some of the components for data management that are required for program quality. The chapter is divided into the following six sections: historically Black colleges and universities (HBCUs) and the EPhD; mission of the EPhD; program overview, objectives, and implementation; alignment and first cohort experiences; and the role of institutional research. In short, institutional research serves a central role in the design, development, and success of this innovative program.

An Academic Innovation: The Executive Ph.D. in Urban Higher Education at a Historically Black University

Joseph Martin Stevenson, Alfredda Hunt Payne

Historically Black Colleges and Universities (HBCUs) and the Executive Ph.D.

The Executive Ph.D. (EPhD) in Urban Higher Education at Jackson State University (JSU) emerged from state-designated funding by the College Board to desegregate higher education and promote social justice, institutional equality, and equitable resource allocation for HBCUs in Mississippi. Jackson State is a HBCU located in the Deep South in Mississippi, one of the poorest areas in the nation. In December 2014, the program celebrated its 10th anniversary. The EPhD is a unique program that has educated, engaged, empowered, and graduated nearly 200 alumni who were or are serving in leadership positions all over America. This program has contributed to the development of effective and efficient leaders at the doctoral level. Most of the students in the first cohort were African American women from HBCUs in Alabama, Arkansas, Georgia, Louisiana, Mississippi, North Carolina, and Texas.

The primary purpose of the EPhD is to educate, at the doctoral level, aspiring, advancing, and actual leaders for the challenges in urban higher

Published online in Wiley Online Library (wileyonlinelibrary.com) • DOI: 10.1002/ir.20163

education from a transdisciplinary context. The "executive" format is very unique and tailored for mid-to-entry–level executives pursuing doctoral education in a rigorous, accelerated, and compressed platform.

The landmark EPhD program has anchored a historical mark in the history of HBCUs. As major contributing knowledge engines to higher education delivery systems in the United States from the mid-to-late 1800s to the present day, HBCUs have played a major fundamental role in not only the African American community but also the historical development of the United States. The United States and, indeed, the world have profited from the intellectual capital, knowledge commodities, neuro development, and cerebral currency that have and continue to evince from the minds, hearts, souls, and hands of graduates of HBCUs (Shults & Stevenson, 2015).

Mission of the EPhD

The EPhD in Urban Higher Education at JSU prepares and develops students to assume senior leadership roles in postsecondary institutions and other organizations whose primary endeavors relate to or impact the operations of higher learning (Jackson State University, n.d.-b). The program actively engages students and faculty in the analysis of the different facets of operations and management of postsecondary institutions. It serves in the development of solutions to potential or existing challenges facing disciplinary perspectives to appreciate the role and impact of these institutions as engines of social and economic change in urban and metropolitan venues.

The academic program consists of a professional specialization core, a higher education core, and coursework in statistics and research. An overview is provided in the Appendix. As illustrated in the Appendix, students master core knowledge in the field of higher education and develop a high level of analytical (quantitative and qualitative research) skills, complemented by an extensive breadth of relevant leadership knowledge in management, planning, and policy. Faculty and administrators associated with the program are committed to the continuous pursuit of "catalytic" knowledge in the discipline of higher education through demonstrated scholarship, outstanding delivery of instruction, and professional service to their fields and the community. The faculty and the founder were advocates of empowering catalysts for positive change, especially in impoverished urban and metropolitan communities that had untapped human potential (Executive Ph.D. in Urban Higher Education, 2016).

The primary program from which the EPhD program was modeled is the Executive Ed.D. program at the University of Pennsylvania. With guidance from the late thought leader, Dr. J. Douglas Toma, who was a former senior fellow at Penn's Graduate School of Education and founding director of the School's Executive Doctorate in Higher Education Management, and Dr. William B. Harvey, currently affiliated with North Carolina Agricultural and Technical State University, initial planning of the EPhD began in 2003.

Back in 2004, the Penn program was found to be the only one in the country that was similar to the EPhD program, although other universities have emulated Jackson State's EPhD and Penn's Ed.D. since 2004. The Ed.D. program at Penn focuses on higher education management; however, a distinct mark of the EPhD program at Jackson State is its transdisciplinary component. Other distinctions between the programs include program length; the EPhD program is 24 months and the Penn Ed.D. program takes slightly less time. The EPhD program is open to students outside the field of higher education.

Program Overview, Objectives, and Implementation

The EPhD prepares faculty and mid-to-entry–level executive personnel in higher education and other related sectors to respond effectively to the challenges posed by metropolitan and urban communities in a pluralistic society undergoing sustained social, economic, and political change. The transdisciplinary degree requires studies in business, public policy and administration, and urban and regional planning in combination with studies in higher education administration, research methodology, and practice.

There was extensive strategic planning for the program as it related to the urban mission of Jackson State University in Jackson, Mississippi—in arguably one of the poorest areas in the world—prior to the program rollout and launch of the EPhD program. During the preplanning stages, the founder and faculty were guided initially by *Curriculum Planning: A Ten Step Process* (Zenger & Zenger, 1982), which succinctly outlined the steps of identifying curriculum need; developing curricular goals and objectives; identifying resources and constraints; organizing a curriculum committee; establishing the roles of human and capital resources; identifying new curriculum (transdisciplinary from business, public policy/administration, urban/regional planning, and higher education leadership); and selecting, designing, implementing, and evaluating new curriculum. This process required extensive and elaborate collaboration with the faculties who represented the disciplines of business, public policy/administration, urban/regional planning, and higher education. Although a somewhat dated source, the Zenger and Zenger work anchored the framework for initiating and implementing the process for program innovation. Other external validation for the EPhD program included an examination of literature on "executive" competencies necessary for successful leadership and other insightful information relevant to urban challenges in higher education.

The following are program objectives developed for the EPhD:

- To provide students with the knowledge, skills, and dispositions required to lead higher education institutions and human service agencies in urban and metropolitan communities.

- To enable students to master the theoretical, conceptual, and research perspectives necessary to improve the quality of life in urban and metropolitan settings.
- To support the development and implementation of clearly defined focused action-research initiatives designed to address existing and pressing urban and metropolitan challenges, such as: (a) pre-K–16 education; (b) human service delivery systems; (c) economic development; (d) urban renewal; (e) regional planning; and (f) individual, group, and community empowerment.
- To create a culture of ongoing intellectual inquiry that supports professional development and lifelong learning (Jackson State University, n.d.-b).

The curriculum of the EPhD program includes the following with the embedded themes and integrated threads of four tenets:

1. Complexity theory—The interdisciplinary exploration of a set of theories from different fields, all of which share focus on complex and adaptive systems and evolution.
2. Exchange analysis—An assessment of overall patterns and system dynamics of value exchange, to determine whether the value-creating system is healthy, sustainable, and expanding.
3. Generative learning—Value-driven learning that seeks what is alive, compelling, and energizing and that expresses a willingness to see radical possibilities beyond the boundaries of current thinking.
4. Community of practice—A group or network of individuals who share a concern, a set of problems, or a passion about a topic, and who deepen their knowledge and expertise in this area by interacting with each other on an ongoing basis (Allee, 2003).

These tenets were extracted from Allee (2003) and vetted for academic relevance by the EPhD founder prior to program launch in 2004 during the 2003 preplanning year. Through the lenses of complexity theory, exchange analysis, generative learning, and community of practice, the EPhD graduates are empowered with the key tools for understanding the social orders from the multidisciplinary context of business, public policy, urban planning, and higher education.

The logic model undergirding the EPhD can be broken up into five fundamental areas to examine prior to the program design and as part of the preplanning and prelaunching process. The first component consisted of "inputs," which are the resources the institution will need in order to implement the program successfully, strategically, and resourcefully. This included best practices and lessons from accreditation standards, finance, personnel, technology, regulatory compliance requirements, campus policies, and procedures. Basically, resources are the areas of institutional capital that provide the foundation for sustainability. The second component included "actions" that describe specifically what will be done with the resources in order to implement the program successfully. There is encouragement to use "action verbs" to describe succinctly what would be done. Words such as *develop*, *create*, *provide*, *encumber*, *employ*, *marshal*, and the like, were used. The third component identified the "outputs," which describe products that are driven from the inputted resources and strategic actions. Often, outputs can be described by numbers or percentages. For instance, the number of courses in higher education will be developed by a specific date with specific resources from the actions. "Outcomes," the fourth component, describe the benefits, impact, dividends, or returns on investments. Outcomes for the EPhD program were conceptualized in the past tense. For instance, the faculty determined that by a certain period in the first year of the degree program, students would have "enhanced" cognition in a specific subject matter. The fifth and final component of the logic model was "assessment," which encompasses planned benchmarks, milestones, measures, metrics, or other performance indicators that are gauged throughout the 2-year degree program.

The EPhD program underwent extensive and elaborate discussion about all five components of the logic model during the incubating stages and early embryonic development of the program. This was a deeply collaborative experience and based on these collegial discussions, a budget for the program was developed prior to launch. The EPhD curriculum was taxonomized, mapped, and refined; the faculty were educated in transdisciplinary relationship building; and other administrative areas were fine-tuned concerning academic operations from the consensus-driven logic model. Thus, from an institutional research perspective, the logic model is a critical area for analysis in an effort to be proactive about securing and sustaining program quality.

Alignment and the First EPhD Cohort

Fundamental to any new academic innovation like the Executive PhD program is the horizontal and vertical alignment of the several matrix relationships, which has produced above-average rates at the recruitment, retention, and graduation levels. First, the program had to be aligned with the institutional mission of Jackson State University, its promulgated strategic goals, and the forward-thinking vision of the founder and the EPhD faculty. Second, the EPhD program was aligned with the strategic competencies and targeted learning expectations of the students. To this end, in the early development of the EPhD program, the faculty and founder embraced the aforementioned four tenets that guided student outcomes, ranging from understanding theoretical constructs within multiple disciplines related to urban leadership to critically and creatively evaluating these constructs against the demands of becoming a "catalyst of positive change" in urban higher and post-secondary education.

Allee's (2003) tenets (complexity theory, exchange analysis, generative learning, and community of practice) were embedded in the program to first anchor the collegial and camaraderie foundation of the cohort model during the program delivery, and second, to build on that collegial camaraderie after the cohort members graduate from the EPhD program to foster networking, peer support, and lifetime connections. These embedded tenets were displayed on the walls, corridors, and classes throughout the center. Third, the EPhD program was aligned with demonstrable and deliverable outcomes for advanced student learning at the doctoral level, and reflected as such in all course syllabi used by the faculty and the students to guide intellectual discourse, deliberation, and disagreement about the future challenges in urban higher education.

Students in the EPhD journey define and develop a quantitative and/or qualitative dissertation topic upon entrance into the program. The program provides its leaders and students with a doctoral experience that is research grounded, transdisciplinary in format and delivery, cohort-based, problem-centered, time bound, fully engaged and immersed, and integrative in nature. With the above in mind, the EPhD program educates and teaches leaders to be capable of managing and motivating people toward solving broad-based metropolitan and urban problems, especially those that emerge in response to dynamic social orders—such as areas like Samford, FL; Ferguson, MO; Baltimore, MD; New York, NY; and Charleston, SC. For example, thought-provoking debates are frequent in the EPhD program—including a spirited debate nearly a decade ago over whether Muslim, Islamic, and Arabic cultures should be infused in college curriculum. Of course, all fundamental areas of these "pro and con" debates were related to the academic goals, competencies, and outcomes for the EPhD program.

To bridge the understanding of urban higher education nationally and globally from formed camaraderie, each cohort participated in one domestic field trip to an urban city, and another trip was to an international urban city. Domestic cities included Birmingham, AL; Memphis, TN; and New York, NY. International cities included Mexico City, Paris, and British Columbia.

In the preplanning stages of the EPhD program, the faculty and founder examined these learning outcomes and strategies through the logic model discussed above. Among the program learning outcomes are: (a) knowledge of theories, issues, and context in higher education leadership; (b) research skills that lead to success of the dissertation; (c) thinking skills that lead to understanding research against issues in higher education; and (d) content knowledge that can be considered for peer presentation or publication. What makes the EPhD different in this regard, given that often PhD programs have similar elements, is the pursuit of these components in an accelerated, compressed, cohort-based, and executive format. To this end, the demonstrable evidence that is assessed against the learning outcomes in the

EPhD program include both in class and online examinations, academic papers, individual and group presentations, tests, or simulations from subject matter subtext, content and context; successful pass rates on comprehensive examinations; dissertation hearings and proposals; and refereed journal publications and conference presentations.

Why Institutional Research Data Were and Are Paramount to the EPhD

The EPhD program is considered one of the most innovative program development initiatives in the HBCU sector—a sector that has made profound contributions with vast returns on investment to American higher education and beyond—"especially in a nation that is focused on outcomes but conveniently forgets the inputs that lead to the outcomes" (Gasman, Castro Samayoa, & Commodore, 2015). The State of Mississippi provided the resources necessary for the EPhD program from desegregation funding. Data and data-driven decision making guided the impetus for the program's development, a key tool supporting programmatic quality and institutional sustainability.

Knowledge gained from institutional research was critical to the design, the development, the implementation, and the assessment of the EPhD program at JSU. Similar to external scanning techniques described in Chapter 2, a market assessment was conducted as part of institutional research by conducting a broader competitor analysis of other PhD programs in higher education. In addition to Penn, this included an examination of programs at the University of California at Los Angeles, the University of Michigan, New York University, Harvard, Stanford, Cambridge, University of Mississippi, Mississippi State, Florida State, and many other research universities. Following the completion of this wide and deep analysis, a tuition rate was identified at a level to be competitive, yet affordable for the program's targeted audience. Other academic market differentiators were examined that allowed the founder and the faculty to develop a specific niche and unique brand for the EPhD. This included program acceleration, weekend offerings, supplemental training in writing and research, career counseling, mentoring, health and wellness guidance, financial planning with financial aid, curriculum developed for professional adults (andragogy), and other areas to support the early refinement of theoretical frameworks for dissertations. Furthermore, institutional research was employed to ensure the program's admission standards are gauged to attract and retain the population targeted for the program. A targeted audience was identified by developing value-added and asset optimization of the EPhD degree.

Other areas that are related to institutional research and data collection were examined during the process of program design and investment. As mentioned earlier, this began with the steps on alignment to confirm that the program is parallel with the mission of the institution and its forecasted strategic plan, as well as the need for the alignment to include a relational connection to the mission and program learning outcomes.

In terms of internal data points, among the areas that are critical to institutional research data are data on student profile and demographics as well as enrollment trends; lessons learned from data on instructional program formats from other higher education programs; best practices and market force data from peer institutions and other benchmarking indicators; data concerning faculty credentials and professorial relevance to the discipline; data on student assessment for learning outcome achievement; and other data relative to program resources concerning technology, library support, fiscal resources, and other resources for maintaining program excellence. Key financial data for budgeting for the program was supported in the institutional research office from close scrutiny of the logic model's inputs with regard to resources. The financials that were a major part of data presented to the institutional research office were generated from both academic and financial administrators at Jackson State University.

The founder also examined literature on success and failure of women and ethnic minorities in doctoral study, along with selected interviews from doctoral graduates from other HBCUs. The results from these data analyses were carefully examined and revealed findings were incorporated into the cohort design of the EPhD program. Results from literature reviews revealed that many doctoral students experience a sense of isolation, a need to plan financially, concern about life balance and health, a need to refine and fine-tune the dissertation proposal, and a need to polish and perfect a writing style that is appropriate for doctoral training. To this end, the program developed the cohort model to build collegial camaraderie. The program also designated a financial aid specialist to work with students. Moreover, the program integrated health modules as well as provided career mentors for students, many of whom were faculty members from the University of Michigan, the University of Georgia, and the University of California. A designated program faculty member was responsible for working with students concerning the appropriate writing style pursuant to the American Psychological Association (APA). The program also included special workshops on refining the dissertation proposal that later resulted in a book published by some of the program faculty, entitled, *"INQUIRY: Investigative Nuances, Questions, and Understandings in Educational Research Yield* (Stevenson, Crockett, Jefferson, Walker, & Warner, 2015).

All of these data pressure points facilitated the planning for sustainable academic quality, demonstrated educational effectiveness, and other areas relevant to regional and program accreditation. The institutional research data were also fundamental to the development of a strategic plan within the context of the institutional mission. Institutional research data were paramount to doctoral programming for gauging student persistence toward degree completion and faculty performance and productivity. This included not only student demographic data, but data concerning retention and graduation rates, time to degree completion, student satisfaction, and other data from alumni surveys and job placement. The Office of Institutional Research also required the faculty and founder to examine the landscape of the workforce in higher education to determine job opportunities for graduates and other areas concerning career placement.

As addressed in Chapter 5, institutional research was also important with regard to the faculty. Data concerning faculty diversity, workload, expertise, and professional development within their discipline complemented data-driven decision making by the program with the aid of institutional research.

Conclusion

In sum, there are many lessons to be learned from the practices at Jackson State University concerning the academic innovation of a doctoral program in urban higher education. First, institutional research and the examination of data must be an early part of the discussions for program innovation—weighing all risks, threats, potential barriers, strengths, assets, and contingencies. Second, program alignment with institutional mission and vision are fundamental to goal attainment. The best way to gauge this is to develop a decision matrix that denotes all of the relationships that are necessary for success. This would include a matrix that encompasses relationship connections between finance, academics, bureaucracy, and infrastructure. Third, institutional research plays a culminating role in the initial and ongoing examination of areas relevant to program investment. This includes program alignment, external validation, academic market assessment, environmental competitor analysis (or scanning), asset market differentiators, workforce demands and needs, resources and capital, and other areas that contribute to recruitment, enrollment, retention, matriculation, graduation, and placement of aspiring leaders in leadership roles throughout urban higher education in the United States.

Given that the EPhD program is the first of its kind in America, and the fact that it was created at a HBCU, this innovation is certain to continue to be a historical source of pride with over 10 cohorts graduated, evidence of the program's past, present, and future contribution to American higher education.

References

Allee, V. (2003). *The future of knowledge: Increasing prosperity through value networks.* Burlington, MA: Elsevier Science.

Executive Ph.D. in Urban Higher Education. (2016). *Welcome.* Retrieved from http://www.jsums.edu/ephd/

Gasman, M., Castro Samayoa, A., & Commodore, F. (2015). Black colleges matter: And we have the data to prove it. *Newsweek*. Retrieved from http://www.newsweek.com/black-colleges-matter-and-we-have-data-prove-it-366306

Jackson State University. (n.d.-a). *Executive Ph.D. in Urban Higher Education. A degree for higher education catalyst in urban communities* [Program brochure] (p. 4). Available from Jackson State University, 1400 J.R. Lynch St., Jackson, MS 39217.

Jackson State University. (n.d.-b). *Jackson State University Graduate Catalog 2003–2007* (p. 67). (n.d.). Available from Jackson State University, 1400 J.R. Lynch St., Jackson, MS 39217.

Shults, C. A., & Stevenson, J. M. (2015). *American treasures: Building, leveraging, and sustaining capacity in historically black colleges and universities*. Palo Alto, CA: Academica Press.

Stevenson, J. M., Crockett, W. L., Jefferson, A. R., Walker, R. E., & Warner, N. (2015). *INQUIRY: Investigative nuances, questions, and understandings in educational research yield*. Palo Alto, CA: Academica Press.

Zenger, W. F., & Zenger, S. K. (1982). *Curriculum planning: A ten step process*. Palo Alto, CA: R & E Research Associates.

Appendix: Academic Program Overview

Professional Specialization Core (18 hours)	*Higher Education Core (15 hours)*	*Statistics and Research Methods (15 hours)*
Seminar in Governmental and Not-for-Profit Accounting Methods of Urban and Regional Analysis and Planning Seminar in Program Development, Implementation, and Evaluation Public Policy Formulation Theoretical Perspectives in Planning and Building Community Groups Ethics in Planning, Change, and Leadership Seminar	Philosophy and History in Higher Education Educational Futures: Planning and Development Seminar in Legal Aspects of Higher Education Educational, Governmental, and Corporate Relationships Higher Education Leadership and Organization in Cross-Culture Environments	Advanced Statistical Methods Qualitative Research Methods Quantitative Research Methods • Research-Based Teaching Methods • Research Seminar: Intellectual Capital/Knowledge Management and Human Resources
Cognate Component (12 hours)	Dissertation (12 hours)	Total 72 hours
Twelve (12) hours from previous graduate work must be approved for transfer before admission is granted to enhance the cognate area of interest and to complement the core.		

JOSEPH MARTIN STEVENSON is the Vice President and Chief Academic Officer at The Chicago School of Professional Psychology.

ALFREDDA HUNT PAYNE is a consultant with the Department of State and the US Agency for International Development.

7

This chapter sheds light on the ways in which institutional research (IR) professionals can be involved in the development and/or modification of high-quality academic programs. Suggestions from authors within this volume for how IR can assist in accomplishing these goals will be integrated and organized in alignment with Terenzini's (1993) three tiers of organizational intelligence.

Making the Connections Across Institutional Types and Academic Programs: Recommendations for Institutional Research Practice and Future Research

Beverly Rae King

The chapters in this volume all speak to the important role that institutional research (IR) professionals can play in academic program planning, development, and revision. Whether programs are developed within a community college (Chapters 1, 3, and 4) or a 4-year university; at the graduate (Chapter 5) or undergraduate level and not-for-profit institutions; or within a minority-serving (Chapter 6) institution, partnering with IR should be a first step for academic program development teams.

Fincher (1978) described IR as *organizational intelligence*. Terenzini (1993) expanded this concept when he identified three levels of organizational intelligence—technical and analytic, issue, and contextual. IR staff display *technical and analytic* intelligence (the most basic of Terenzini's tiers) when they pull and provide data on faculty, students, staff, and facilities at their institutions, or when they utilize computer software to present or analyze the numbers. *Issues intelligence* consists of knowledge of the issues (primarily internal) facing a given institution, knowledge of how decisions are made, and the ability to identify and work with key people to address those issues. At the top of the organizational intelligence hierarchy is *contextual intelligence*, which includes an understanding of the culture of higher education, how business is conducted at one's institution, and knowledge of the external trends (demographic, financial, social, or political) likely to have an impact on higher education in general or on one's own institution specifically. Further discussion of Terenzini's tiers is provided in Volkwein, Liu, and Woodell (2012), and Eimers, Ko, and Gardner (2012).

Although technical and analytic intelligence is often seen as the key feature of an IR office, staff within these offices are uniquely situated to understand internal issues and monitor external trends. That is, few other offices in a college or university are able to see the institution from the "bird's eye" view available to the IR practitioner. Authors Freeman, Chambers, and Newton (Chapter 5) reinforce this observation when they point out that "... institutional research offices offer quality internships given their unique position overseeing all university units and processes." In fact, through the process of partnering with IR in the form of graduate student interns, faculty and other higher education practitioners can obtain a clearer picture of the role of their own units within the university at large.

The importance of the IR vantage point is also illustrated in Chapter 2 by Goodchild, Chambers, and Freeman, as they discuss the roles that environmental scanning and institutional SWOT (strengths, weaknesses, opportunities, and threats) analyses can play in the development of distinctive academic programs. The remainder of the current chapter will be devoted to outlining the types of data, information, and skills that IR can provide to and for academic programmers with the use of examples culled from the chapters in this volume and organized by Terenzini's (1993) tiers of organizational intelligence.

Contributions of IR to Academic Program Development/Revision

Technical and Analytic Intelligence. Data and analyses on students and faculty in existing programs can be utilized for the purpose of planning program expansion, or other revisions such as transitioning a program to online delivery, updating a program's curriculum, or combining programs. The authors in this volume have suggested the following data and analyses, but many more could be added to the list: Data on program applicants, such as the number of applicants, acceptance rate, and yield; current student profiles; student and alumni survey results; student credit hour production; enrollment trends and projected enrollments at the institution, division, and program levels; learning outcome assessment results; retention, graduation, and job-placement rates; time-to-degree analyses; and faculty workload/productivity. Data and analyses that support academic program development often include comparisons among institutions with similar programs; thus, IR's familiarity with the Integrated Postsecondary Education Data System (IPEDS) Data Center tools can be invaluable. IR staff may supply program developers with data obtained from IPEDS, such as degrees awarded in similar programs at peer institutions, or provide a "how-to" guide with step-by-step instructions so that program developers can explore

IPEDS data on their own. As program developers explore these and other data resources relevant to their proposals, IR liaisons also can assist with "translating" terminology that is not as familiar outside of IR as within, for instance, instructional program codes or related occupational and industry-level codes.

Issues Intelligence. Recall that issues intelligence consists of knowledge of internal issues as well as key people and how decisions are made. As one of the primary tasks of IR offices is to provide data and information to key decision makers within the college or university, it behooves IR staff to understand the decision context within the institution, as discussed by Dee and Heineman in Chapter 1. Decision context includes not only the type of decision to be made and its scope but also the institution's history in making that type of decision and stages in decision development.

IR can provide assistance in academic program development with the use of issues intelligence in a number of ways. One obvious example is in helping program planners interpret data with an eye toward institutional and programmatic issues. Other ways, as enumerated in this volume include facilitating communication, helping academic program planners connect their proposals to the institution's strategic plan, and assessing institutional capacity, to name just a few. Of course, the particular ways in which IR utilizes its intelligence is dependent upon how each IR office is structured and the function for which it is responsible.

One challenge to academic program development is "fragmented communication and limited coordination across departmental boundaries" (Dee & Heineman, Chapter 1). IR professionals, especially IR directors, interact with and come to know faculty and staff in a wide variety of academic departments and functional units on a campus. With that exposure and knowledge, they can serve as communication facilitators, bringing together people and ideas in a way that is not possible for faculty and staff whose primary interactions are within their own departments or units.

Dee and Heineman also observe that "[c]onnecting academic program proposals to the [university] strategic plan is important because at many institutions, administrators allocate resources based on the extent to which a proposed initiative can contribute to the institution's strategic priorities." If, as Freeman, Chambers, and Newton (Chapter 5) observe ". . .academic planning is the heart and soul of an institution's overall strategic plan," then IR professionals who play a role in helping to formulate or track the success of an institution's strategic plan have a responsibility to assist academic planners in understanding that plan and tying its components to their proposals. Goodchild, Chambers, and Freeman (Chapter 2) emphasize the importance of SWOT analyses to program development. Many universities utilize the SWOT technique in strategic planning; IR offices can not only participate in SWOT analyses, they can lead efforts to translate the results of SWOT analyses into actionable strategic plan components, including ways for universities to develop distinctive academic programs.

Another way in which IR can assist in academic program development as addressed in several chapters in this volume (Chapters 1 and 5) is in the assessment of institutional capacity. Assessing capacity to support a new or expanding program is not an easy task, and institutions may vary in their definitions or categorization of "capacity." In general, however, capacity assessment might include analyzing and integrating current and forecasted information on institutional mission, infrastructure, number and expertise of faculty, leadership support, technology support, and financial opportunities/constraints.

Contextual Intelligence. IR offices whose staff do not engage in regular environmental scanning are doing themselves and their institutions a disservice. Important developments that will impact higher education should be monitored at the local, regional, and national levels. Critical to high-quality academic program proposals is taking into account trends (again, locally, regionally, and nationally) in programs offered at other institutions, enrollment and degrees awarded in these programs, and what the job market is (and will be) for graduates. Goodchild, Chambers, and Freeman (Chapter 2) assert the criticality of environmental scanning to, and provide examples of how it has played a role in, strategic planning of distinctive academic programs. Both the authors of Chapter 1 (Dee and Heineman) and those of Chapter 6 (Stevenson and Payne) emphasize the significant role that labor market data and projections can play in academic program development. Resources include the National Employment Matrix database and the Occupational Projections database, both maintained by the United States Bureau of Labor Statistics (http://www.bls.gov/).

Calderone and Webber (2013) envision a shift of Terenzini's (1993) framework of organizational intelligence within IR over the next two decades, with less focus on the first tier (technical and analytical intelligence) and more on the second and third tiers (issues and contextual intelligence). IR professionals will increasingly be called upon not just to supply numbers, but also to serve as consultants and advisors in how to interpret and use data in the service of institutional effectiveness and efficiency. The current volume particularly encourages partnerships between IR and academic planners in the service of robust programs that prepare students for successful college and career experiences. Collaborations such as these can not only aid the student experience but also contribute to the "desiloization" of academia and increase the knowledge base of all involved.

References

Calderone, A., & Webber, K. L. (2013). Institutional research in the future: Challenges within higher education and the need for excellence in professional practice. In A. Calderone & K. L. Webber (Eds.), *Global Issues in Institutional Research. New Directions in Institutional Research*, 157, 77–90.

Eimers, M. T., Ko, J. W., & Gardner, D. (2012). Practicing institutional research. In Howard, McLaughlin, Knight, and associates (Eds.), *Handbook of institutional research* (pp. 40–56). San Francisco, CA: Jossey-Bass.
Fincher, C. (1978). Institutional research as organizational intelligence. *Research in Higher Education*, *8*(2), 189–192.
Terenzini, P. (1993). On the nature of institutional research and the knowledge and skills it requires. *Research in Higher Education*, *34*(1), 1–10.
Volkwein, J. F., Liu, Y.(J.), & Woodell, J. (2012). The structure and functions of institutional research offices. In Howard, McLaughlin, Knight, and associates (Eds.), *Handbook of institutional research* (pp. 22–39). San Francisco, CA: Jossey-Bass.

Beverly Rae King is the Director of Institutional Research at East Carolina University.

Index